NATHAN BEDFORD FORREST AND AFRICAN-AMERICANS

Yankee Myth, Confederate Fact

LOCHLAINN SEABROOK WRITES IN THE FOLLOWING GENRES

Adult	Matriarchy
Alternate History	Men
American Civil War	Metaphysics
American History	Military History
American Politics	Mysteries and Enigmas
American South	Mysticism
Ancient History	Natural Health
Anthropology	Natural History
Apocrypha	Onomastics
Aviation	Paleography
Biblical Exegesis	Paleontology
Biblical Hermeneutics	Paranormal
Biography	Patriarchy
Children	Philosophy
Christian Mysticism	Photography
Coffee Table	Pictorial
Comparative Mythology	Poetry
Comparative Religion	Politics
Cooking	Prehistory
Cryptozoology	Presidential History
Diet and Nutrition	Quiz
Education	Reference
Encyclopediology	Religion
Entertainment	Revolutionary Period
Ethnic Studies	Science
Etymology	Scripture
European History	Self-help
Evolutionary Biology	Social Sciences
Exposés	Spirituality
Family Histories	Spiritualism
Film	Sport Science
Genealogy	Technology
Ghost Stories	Thanatology
Gospels	Thealogy
Health and Fitness	Theology
Historical Fiction	UFOlogy
Historical Nonfiction	Vexillology
History	Victorian Period
Humanities	War
Humor	Western
Illustrations	Wildlife
Law of Attraction	Women
Lexicography	World History
Life After Death	Young Adult

Mr. Seabrook does not author books for fame and glory, but for the love of writing and sharing his knowledge.

Be curious, not judgmental.

NATHAN BEDFORD FORREST AND AFRICAN-AMERICANS

Yankee Myth, Confederate Fact

LOCHLAINN SEABROOK

JEFFERSON DAVIS HISTORICAL GOLD MEDAL WINNER

**LAVISHLY ILLUSTRATED
EXTENSIVELY RESEARCHED**

Sea Raven Press, Nashville, Tennessee, USA

NATHAN BEDFORD FORREST & AFRICAN-AMERICANS: YANKEE MYTH, CONFEDERATE FACT

Published by
Sea Raven Press, LLC, founded 1995
Nashville, Tennessee, USA
SeaRavenPress.com

Copyright © 2016 Lochlainn Seabrook
in accordance with U.S. and international copyright laws and regulations, as stated and protected under the Berne Union for the Protection of Literary and Artistic Property (Berne Convention), and the Universal Copyright Convention (the UCC). All rights reserved under the Pan-American and International Copyright Conventions.

1st SRP paperback edition, 1st printing: February 2016, ISBN: 978-1-943737-25-3
1st SRP hardcover edition, 1st printing: December 2016, ISBN: 978-1-943737-42-0

ISBN: 978-1-943737-25-3 (paperback)
Library of Congress Control Number: 2016931390

This work is the copyrighted intellectual property of Lochlainn Seabrook and has been registered with the Copyright Office at the Library of Congress in Washington, D.C., USA. No part of this work (including text, covers, drawings, photos, illustrations, maps, images, diagrams, etc.), in whole or in part, may be used, reproduced, stored in a retrieval system, or transmitted, in any form or by any means now known or hereafter invented, without written permission from the publisher. The sale, duplication, hire, lending, copying, digitalization, or reproduction of this material, in any manner or form whatsoever, is also prohibited, and is a violation of federal, civil, and digital copyright law, which provides severe civil and criminal penalties for any violations.

Nathan Bedford Forrest and African-Americans: Yankee Myth, Confederate Fact, by Lochlainn Seabrook.
Includes an index, endnotes, and bibliographical references.

*Front and back cover design and art, book design, layout, and interior art by Lochlainn Seabrook.
All images, graphic design, graphic art, and illustrations copyright © Lochlainn Seabrook.
Cover image: "Forrest and One of His 65 Black Soldiers," by Lochlainn Seabrook.©
Portions of this book have been adapted from the author's other works*

The views on the American "Civil War" documented in this book are those of the publisher.

The paper used in this book is acid-free and lignin-free. It has been certified by the Sustainable Forestry Initiative and the Forest Stewardship Council and meets all ANSI standards for archival quality paper.

PRINTED & MANUFACTURED IN OCCUPIED TENNESSEE, FORMER CONFEDERATE STATES OF AMERICA

DEDICATION

To the 65 black Confederate soldiers, "Old Confeds," who served in Forrest's cavalry, as well as the countless hundreds of others from various units who came under his command during Lincoln's War. I salute them in appreciation of their bravery and their fidelity to the great Southern Cause: constitutional freedom.

EPIGRAPH

This is a proud day for me. . . . I take this occasion to say that I am your friend. I am here as the representative of the Southern people—one that has been more maligned than any other. I assure you that everyman who was in the Confederate army is your friend. We were born on the same soil, breathe the same air, live in the same land, and why should we not be brothers and sisters.

NATHAN BEDFORD FORREST
A Speech Before An All-Black Group
July 4, 1875

CONTENTS

Notes to the Reader - 9
Introduction, by Lochlainn Seabrook - 17

1 FORREST & RACISM - 21
2 FORREST & SLAVERY - 31
3 FORREST & BLACK CONFEDERATE SOLDIERS - 41
4 FORREST & THE BATTLE OF FORT PILLOW - 53
5 FORREST & THE KU KLUX KLAN - 67
6 FORREST & AFRICAN-AMERICANS IN SUMMARY - 81

Appendix A: Gen. N. B. Forrest in 1864 - 89
Appendix B: Gen. N. B. Forrest & the Battle of Fort Pillow - 93
Appendix C: Gen. N. B. Forrest Monument at Rome, GA - 95
Appendix D: The Forrest Equestrian Monument at Memphis, TN - 99
Appendix E: A Brief Biography of Nathan Bedford Forrest - 107
Notes - 109
Bibliography - 113
Index - 118
Meet the Author - 123

NOTES TO THE READER

THE TWO MAIN POLITICAL PARTIES IN 1860
☞ In any study of America's antebellum, bellum, and postbellum periods, it is vitally important to understand that in 1860 the two major political parties—the Democrats and the newly formed Republicans—were the opposite of what they are today. In other words, the Democrats of the mid 19th Century were Conservatives, akin to the Republican Party of today, while the Republicans of the mid 19th Century were Liberals, akin to the Democratic Party of today.

Thus the Confederacy's Democratic president, Jefferson Davis, was a Conservative (with libertarian leanings); the Union's Republican president, Abraham Lincoln, was a Liberal (with socialistic leanings). This is why, in the mid 1800s, the conservative wing of the Democratic Party was known as "the States' Rights Party."[1]

The author's cousin, Confederate Vice President and Democrat Alexander H. Stephens: a Southern Conservative.

Hence, the Democrats of the Civil War period referred to themselves as "conservatives," "confederates," "anti-centralists," or "constitutionalists" (the latter because they favored strict adherence to the original Constitution—which tacitly guaranteed states' rights—as created by the Founding Fathers), while the Republicans called themselves "liberals," "nationalists," "centralists," or "consolidationists" (the latter three because they wanted to nationalize the central government and consolidate political power in Washington, D.C.).[2]

Since this idea is new to most of my readers, let us further demystify it by viewing it from the perspective of the American Revolutionary War. If Davis and his conservative Southern constituents (the Democrats of 1861) had been alive in 1775, they would have sided with George Washington and the American colonists, who sought to secede from the tyrannical government of Great Britain; if Lincoln and his Liberal Northern constituents (the Republicans of 1861) had been alive at that time, they would have sided with King George III and the English monarchy, who sought to maintain the American colonies as possessions of the British Empire. It is due to this very comparison that Southerners often refer to the "Civil War" as the Second American Revolutionary War.[3]

THE TERM "CIVIL WAR"
☞ As I heartily dislike the phrase "Civil War," its use throughout this book (as well as in my other works) is worthy of an explanation.

Today America's entire literary system refers to the conflict of 1861 using the Northern term the "Civil War," whether we in the South like it or not. Thus, as all book searches by readers, libraries, and retail outlets are now performed online, and as all bookstores categorize works from this period under the heading "Civil War," book publishers and authors who deal with this particular topic have little choice but to use this term themselves. If I were to refuse to use it, as some of my Southern colleagues have suggested, few people would ever find or read my books.

Add to this the fact that scarcely any non-Southerners have ever heard of the names we in the South use for the conflict, such as the "War for Southern Independence"—or my personal preference, "Lincoln's War." It only makes sense then to use the term "Civil War" in most commercial situations, distasteful though it is.

We should also bear in mind that while today educated

The American "Civil War" was not a true civil war as Webster defines it: "a conflict between opposing groups of citizens of the same country." It was a fight between two individual countries; or to be more specific, two separate and constitutionally formed confederacies: the U.S.A. and the C.S.A.

persons, particularly educated Southerners, all share an abhorrence for the phrase "Civil War," it was not always so. Confederates who lived through and even fought in the conflict regularly used the term throughout the 1860s, and even long after. Among them were Confederate generals such as Nathan Bedford Forrest, Richard Taylor, and Joseph E. Johnston, not to mention the Confederacy's vice president, Alexander H. Stephens.

In 1895 Confederate General James Longstreet wrote about his military experiences in a work subtitled, *Memoirs of the Civil War in America*. Even the Confederacy's highest leader, President Jefferson Davis, used the term "Civil War,"[4] and in one case at least, as late as 1881—the year he wrote his brilliant exposition, *The Rise and Fall of the Confederate Government*.[5]

ON THE WORD "RACE"

☞ As with the phrase "Civil War," I use the word "race" only as a concession to popular culture. As genetic studies have repeatedly shown, there is no such thing as a separate or "pure" race of people. In other words, there is no gene that makes one "red" (Indian), "yellow" (Asian), "white" (European), "black" (African), or "brown" (Hispanic). All living humans are simply "varieties" that descend from a single ancestor, belong to a single race, derive their genes from a single source, and form a single species: *Homo sapiens sapiens*.[6]

More scientifically, every member of our species shares the

same number of chromosomes, is inter-fertile with all others, and has blood that is constructed of the identical pattern of agglutinins and antigens—which is what makes blood transfusions between *all* humans possible.[7] Even many of our more enlightened ancient predecessors understood this, one of whom was Saint Paul, who said:

> God that made the world and all things therein . . . hath made of one blood all nations of men for to dwell on all the face of the earth.[8]

The widely varied appearances of humans stem not only from heredity (our ancestors), but also from geographic, that is, environmental, conditions. Thus physically speaking we are primarily the products of that part of the world in which our ancestors lived. This means, in turn, that there are no "superior" or "inferior" races, as individuals such as Yankee President Abraham Lincoln and Yankee Generals Ulysses S. Grant and William T. Sherman believed.[9]

For example, prehistoric people who lived in cold dark climates tended to have short stocky bodies, straight hair, small narrow noses, blue eyes, and light skin, all physical adaptations to cool temperatures, low humidity, upper elevations, and decreased sunlight—that is, boreal environments. Prehistoric people who lived in warm sunny climates tended to have tall thin bodies, curly hair, large broad noses, brown eyes, and dark skin, in this case all physical adaptations to hot temperatures, high humidity, low elevations, and increased sunlight—that is, equatorial environments. All humans descend from recent and distant ancestors that were from one or both of these geographical regions (or from regions that lie between them), which explains the immensely diverse physical traits of the human species.

Confounding both popular belief and science, there are exceptions, even reversals, to this rule, such as instances in which white children have been born to black parents with no known

Caucasian ancestry, and black children who have been born to white parents with no known African ancestry.[10] And since some whites become quite dark from sun exposure while some do not, and since blacks have dark skin in all environments, we know that it is not just heredity that determines traits like skin color. It is the way an individual reacts to his environment—and it is *this* particular trait that is inherited.[11]

British anthropologist Ashley Montagu has called the idea of race "man's most dangerous myth," for it catalogs people not merely by physically distinguishable populations, but by the common belief that these differences are inherently connected to higher or lower mental capacities, capacities that can allegedly be measured by both cultural achievements and IQ tests.[12] Yet no such measurement can be taken because no such link exists. "Race" then is one of those ideas that lies beyond infallible systemization; it is a nonsensical and thus worthless concept that "deifies all attempts at classification."[13]

Cheyenne Chief Wolf Robe (pictured here) is commonly referred to as a "Native-American." Spiritually and genetically speaking, however, there is no such thing, making this term, like all other racial nomenclature, useless and misleading. Not only is the soul race-less (Galatians 3:28), the apparent physical differences between people are nothing more than evolutionary adaptations resulting from where our ancestors once lived. There is only one race: the human race; a great inter-fertile group in which every member shares the same number of chromosomes, identical blood substances, and the same taxonomic family name: *homo sapiens sapiens*. The sooner racists, whatever their color, understand and accept this fact, the better.

In a word, human beings are simply not capable of being arranged into clear-cut categories, for there are far too many variables, from natural selection and environmental adaptation, to genetic mutations and the random modification of hereditary characters. The massive genetic diversity resulting from these sporadic, spontaneous, and often unknowable and untraceable influences makes the very concept of a "pure race" impossible.[14]

Indeed, the "diversity" of the human species is much smaller than popular culture imagines: the female eggs that created the world's present human population would all fit inside a one gallon jar, while the sperm cells that produced us would easily fit into an aspirin tablet. In fact, the hereditary material that formed all living human beings would only take up the space of one large multivitamin.[15]

The word "race" then turns out to be an invented construct, an arbitrary and convenient term that has no relationship to biology (skin color, hair and facial characteristics, body type, etc.), culture, religion, linguistics, or nationality. This, in turn, renders the concept of "racism" pointless, which is why the word race has been slowly disappearing from science books for many decades. Anthropologists, for instance, no longer classify humans by skin color, but rather by biological and genetic variability and the influence of these factors on different populations that are far more accurately called "ethnic groups" or "genogroups," rather than "races."[16] Anything else must be labeled false science and illogical theorizing based on faulty misconceptions about human biology.[17]

In truth what "racist" blacks do not like about non-Africans, what "racist" browns do not like about non-Hispanics, what "racist" yellows do not like about non-Asians, what "racist" reds do not like about non-Indians, and what "racist" whites do not like about non-Europeans, is, in almost all cases, social and cultural, not "racial."

Furthermore, if one is biased toward another due to their appearance, this is lookism, not racism. If one is biased toward another because of their age, this is ageism, not racism. If one is biased toward another due to their gender, this is sexism, not racism. All of these "isms" have, at one time or another, been misinterpreted and mischaracterized as "racism." Hence, I have put forth a replacement word for racism, *socioculturalism*: prejudice toward an individual or group based on their social or cultural background and conditions.

While it is doubtless time to rid our language of the ambiguous, artificial, obsolete, generalized, loaded, stereotyping, imprecise, limited, mystical, and meaningless word "race" and its "built-in confusion,"[18] I continue to use it, in this book because—as there is yet no public consensus agreement on an alternate—my word "socioculturalism" would only confuse my readers.

LANGUAGE
☞ Liberals find the use of the terms "reds" (for Native-Americans), "browns" (for Hispanic-Americans), "blacks" (for African-Americans), and "yellows" (for Asian-Americans) "embarrassing." Yet they use the term "whites," usually in a disparaging manner, for anyone who is not Indian, Hispanic, African, or Asian. Thus, to be both fair and non-biased, where necessary I use the words reds, browns, blacks, and yellows for the various ethnogroups, including the word whites for European-Americans.

TO LEARN MORE
☞ Lincoln's War on the American people and the Constitution can never be fully understood without a thorough knowledge of the South's perspective. As this book is only meant to be a brief introductory guide to General Forrest and African-Americans, one cannot hope to learn the whole truth about the War here. For those who are interested in a more in-depth study, please see my comprehensive histories listed on page 2.

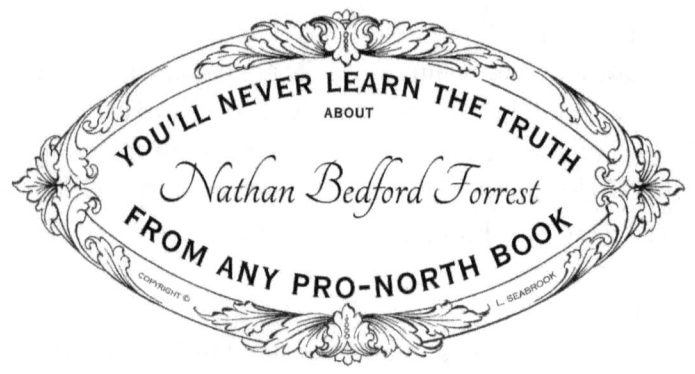

INTRODUCTION

I have traveled and lived all over the U.S. and have never come across a single instance of white racism, *except in the North*. In the South, where my Kentucky family traces its lineage back to America's first permanent English settlement, Jamestown, Virginia (1607), and where I have spent the majority of my life, I have never known or even heard of a white racist.

To the contrary, every white Southerner in my experience has been the epitome of egalitarianism, evincing nothing but acceptance, respect, and even a predilection for nonwhite races. I believe nearly all Southerners, whatever their skin color, will agree with me on this. If one is seeking the closest thing to a racial utopia in the U.S., away from prejudice, narrow-mindedness, and discrimination, he or she could no better than to move to the American South.

My views and experiences should not be surprising: though you will never read this in any mainstream history book, the truth is that the American abolition movement got its start in the South, while both the American slave trade and American slavery got their start in the North.

Alexis de Tocqueville, 19th-Century French political philosopher, was only one of countless individuals who visited the U.S. and discovered that white racism was much more profound and entrenched in the North than in the South, and that white Southerners were more racially tolerant and accepting than their Yankee counterparts. The same holds true to this day, but the anti-South movement would rather you not know this.

This is precisely why 18th- and 19th-Century visitors to the U.S., like French diplomat and historian Alexis de Tocqueville, found white racism to be greater and deeper in the North than in the South. This is why blacks were barred from Abraham Lincoln's funeral, but were welcomed at Jefferson Davis' funeral. And this is why white racism and white hate crimes are still far more common in the realm of the Yankee than anywhere else in the U.S.

Love of the truth is universal, which is why African-Americans all over the U.S. read, recommend, sell, and enthusiastically promote the author's literary works about Lincoln's War. Above Karen Cooper of the Virginia Flaggers holds Lochlainn Seabrook's bestselling book, *Everything You Were Taught About the Civil War is Wrong, Ask a Southerner!* Ms. Karen wrote the foreword to Mr. Seabrook's equally popular work, *Give This Book to a Yankee! A Southern Guide to the Civil War for Northerners*.

Irrespective of these bold facts, our left-leaning historians expect us to believe that white Southerners who lived during the Civil War were "die-hard racists," while white Northerners were "the paragons of racial tolerance and love"—ideas that, as I will show, are not only irrational in the extreme, but fly in the face of authentic history.

The white Southerner these self-appointed "guardians of American history" long ago chose to best embody their fabricated "Southern racism" was none other than Confederate General Nathan Bedford Forrest. Why? For one thing, he is rightly considered one of the South's most lauded and esteemed heroes, and thus smearing him is guaranteed to stir up Southern emotion, while at the same time allowing one of Dixie's most beloved icons to be savagely disparaged, incriminated, and misrepresented.[19]

But there is another reason Forrest is the Left's favorite whipping post. He was the archetypal Southerner: not only was he of European descent (as of 2016, now an often oppressed minority in at least four American states),[20] he was also a staunch Conservative, constitutionalist, and Christian, who embraced traditional American, family, and religious values; values for which Liberals have long had nothing but disdain and antipathy.

How different Southern fact is from Northern mythology!

Was Forrest truly a vile bigot? Was he really a violent brute who detested the very sight of African-Americans, and beat, tortured, and murdered them "at every opportunity"? Was he, in fact, the barbaric slaver that Yankee historians say he was, a sadistic monster who "molested his black slave girls" and "beat his black male slaves to death with chains"?

No Southerner has been so flagrantly, dishonestly, and violently defamed as Nathan Bedford Forrest. Yet not one word of this mountain of intentionally manufactured slander is true.

Was his famous cavalry unit comprised solely of fellow white supremacists, who "spent the entire Civil War hunting down and killing African-Americans"? Was he actually the "founder and first leader of the Ku Klux Klan" and the bloodthirsty "Butcher of Fort Pillow," as our progressive textbooks solemnly declare? Was Forrest really comparable to Jack the Ripper, Mussolini, and even Hitler, as many modern whites and blacks still believe?

As I will show in the following pages, not only are none of these views and accusations true, they are the complete opposite of reality.

For those in search of the facts about Nathan Bedford Forrest and African-Americans, read on. This book will help reestablish the Truth about the highly venerated Rebel chieftain and the nonwhite races, thereby restoring him to his rightful and honored place on the stage of American history.

Hand this book out freely to Forrest-haters, South-loathers, and racists (of all colors), in particular to uninformed politicians, educators, and social leaders who are still living in the Stone Age of radical Left-wing ideology. It will totally transform their views of both Forrest and the American South.

Lochlainn Seabrook
Nashville, Tennessee, USA
February 2016

1

FORREST & RACISM

CRITICS OF NATHAN BEDFORD FORREST claim that he was a racist, and that for this reason alone his name should be erased from our history books, all of his statues torn down, his image banned from the public arena, and every Forrest school, Forrest park, and Forrest historic site renamed in honor of someone "whose name is not synonymous with evil."

To these ill-informed individuals Forrest was not just a racist. He was a *vicious* racist whose hatred of African-Americans was only restrained by the law; the promulgator of a violent bigotry fueled by rabid white supremacist and white separatist sentiments, the same views that later prompted him to "found and lead the Ku Klux Klan."

Despite the fact that these accusations are demonstrably erroneous and obviously purposefully fabricated to smear Forrest's reputation and insult and provoke the South, pro-North writers continue to churn them out year after year, masquerading them as "genuine history." Sadly, for a century and a half the public has been taken in by these rank falsehoods, and now, as a Southern historian, it is my responsibility to debunk them.

Let us start at the beginning.

Forrest was born at a time when racism was an accepted worldwide reality. Though the Left-wing authors of our history books and textbooks would rather you not know the truth, racism was common and endemic to *all* races in the past, just as it is still found to a lesser or greater extent among *all* races today.

Many are not aware of this because black, red, brown, and yellow racism (both past and present) are all carefully filtered out of public view by the Liberal media. According to its one-sided rules, only white racism is allowed to be portrayed or discussed on TV, in film, in books, magazine articles, on the radio, and on the Internet. In the Liberal's mind, there is no such thing as nonwhite racism, for reds, blacks, browns, and yellows are "incapable of being racist."

This silly proposition is motivated by something far more serious, however: a progressive, global, anti-white movement that seeks to devalue, demonize, and marginalize anything European—particularly anyone of European descent, like Nathan Bedford Forrest. This overt racism is most evident in those who claim to be the most nonracist, a phenomenon they themselves are wholly oblivious to.

The Nez Percé Indians were ardent slavers, not only of fellow reds, but of whites, blacks, and browns as well. Red racism toward blacks and especially whites was and still is common, but is never mentioned by our liberal historians, progressive educators, or our leftist-controlled media.

Yet, a ubiquitous and deeply entrenched racism exists among all races, whether it offends Liberals or not. As the following examples illustrate, we need only scratch beneath the surface of what I call "The Great Yankee Coverup" to find it.[21]

- Sitting Bull, chief of the Dakota Sioux, once said that "there was never an Indian who did not hate whites."[22]

- The Klamath Indian word for blacks is *niggalam shaamoksh*, the term for "monkey."[23]
- Native-American racism toward whites is known to be common on modern Indians reservations.[24]
- From at least the 1600s on, African-Americans viewed European-Americans as an "inferior race" due to their white skin—a vestige of the native African belief that "only black skin is beautiful."[25]
- Racism within the Native-American and African-American communities themselves toward their own darker skinned compatriots has long been known and discussed.[26]
- Among Asian-Americans a host of racist words have long been used for whites. The Cantonese, for example, use the word *gweilo*, which loosely translated means "foreign devil."[27]

This list is endless, and indeed, volumes could be written on nonwhite racism both in the U.S. and worldwide. The point is that racism in early America was omnipresent and was found among all the nonwhite races—*and still is.*

Concerning white racism specifically, little needs to be said about it because—thanks to our Leftist history books—it is already well-known. In fact, because this is the only kind of racial prejudice most authors write about, many people falsely believe that there is no other kind of racism.[28] This problem also stems from the fact that white American racism has been with us since the late 1400s, when a racist European named Christopher Columbus began slaughtering and enslaving Native-Americans by the millions.

Columbus' racial crimes left their mark on white American society: by the 1800s European-Americans were viewing Africans as a "missing link" or primitive "bridge" between apes and humans, one that was so evolutionarily feeble that the race would one day "die out" in the U.S.[29]

Early American white racism was the most pronounced and

most severe, however, not in the South, as we have been taught, but in the North, as countless visitors to both sections noted in the 1800s. No one personified Yankee racism more profoundly than big government Liberal, President Abraham Lincoln.

U.S. President Abraham Lincoln was the archetypal white Northern racist, white Northern supremacist, and white Northern separatist; one who continually impeded the social progress of blacks and who, as a member and leader of the racist Yankee organization, the American Colonization Society, spent his entire adult life trying to come up with a plan to deport African-Americans "back to their native land," as he stated in his public speeches.

It was Dishonest Abe who frequently called blacks "niggers," who consistently blocked black civil rights, who stalled emancipation, who backed the 1861 Corwin Amendment (that would have allowed American slavery to continue in perpetuity), who banned blacks from entering the White House, who used slave labor to finish constructing the Capitol Building, and who issued racist military policies that outraged both black civil rights leaders and white abolitionists. It was also Lincoln who referred to all nonwhites as "inferior races," Indians as "savages," and Mexicans as "mongrels" and "greasers." This was the same man who was proud to be a black colonizationist, one who spent his entire adult life trying to find ways to ship all African-Americans "back to their native land," as he put it in a speech October 16, 1854.[30]

Because he was a Liberal and a Northerner, however, our leftist historians are not interested in Lincoln's racism and would rather you not know about it. And so they conveniently leave it out of our history books. What they *are* interested in—and are actually obsessed with—is *Southern* racism, and more specifically

Forrest's racism, which they never cease to delight in discussing.

But was he the racist that pro-North writers say he was? Let us examine what Forrest himself had to say on the subject. As we will see, his racism was far less acute and dangerous than Lincoln's, or any other Northerner for that matter.

Once when asked what he thought of giving blacks the right to vote, Forrest made it clear that he supported the idea, that he was not against blacks, and that, in fact, skin color was of no concern to him:

> We will stand by those who help us. And here I want you to understand distinctly I am not an enemy to the negro. We want him here among us; he is the only laboring class we have; and, more than that, I would sooner trust him than the white scalawag [a white anti-South Southerner] or carpet-bagger [a white anti-South Northerner].[31]

Obviously, from this statement alone, it is clear that completely contrary to Northern myth, Forrest was a friend of African-Americans, not their foe. As we will see, not only did he free all of his slaves either before or during Lincoln's War, he happily hired hundreds of free blacks afterward.

During a postwar examination on the witness stand before a Yankee committee, Forrest spoke of the 400 freedmen he employed on his railroad—not just as laborers, but also as architects, engineers, conductors, and foremen, occupations that were still closed to blacks in most of New England at the time. Though the General was considered a "racist" by many in the racist North, Southerners knew the truth. As we are about to see, after his black rail employees' one-year contract ran out, all but 15 returned to continue working for him—unlikely if he was a bigot.[32]

This topic came up when the panel asked the General if his black workers were allowed to "vote as they please," insinuating that Southerners like Forrest were forcing their black employees to vote Democratic (then the Conservative Party). He replied:

They voted as they pleased at the last election. About three hundred had come from North Carolina, but they were not entitled to vote; had not been in Alabama long enough; they had been working a portion of the time in Mississippi, and they did not vote. But *all those who were entitled to vote voted without any molestation. I said when I started out with my roads that railroads had no politics; that I wanted the assistance of everybody; that railroads were for the general good of the whole country. We have had no political discussion along the line of my road; we have had no difficulty. I hired three hundred colored men in North Carolina, and they worked for me twelve months*; their time was out last May; they were paid off. *About one hundred and fifty of them returned*, and a portion of them, in fact I think about fifteen, have come back. They got one-half of their money monthly until the end of the year, when they were paid off.[33]

All of the accusations concerning General Forrest's alleged racism melt away like morning dew before the sun when the facts are examined honestly and objectively. Only the illiterate and uninformed continue to embrace this type of preposterous and conspicuous anti-South propaganda—invented expressly to smear Forrest and humiliate the conservative Christian South.

Again, from this it is plain that the North has long portrayed Forrest as an intransigent racist merely to sabotage his reputation, embarrass the South, and carry on the fake "race war" created by 19th-Century Liberals—one still being perpetuated by skin-color obsessed Liberals today.[34]

Sadly, to a great extent this ploy has worked. To this day, a majority of people—even in the South—associate Forrest's name with racism. This despite the fact that he was, unlike Lincoln and most other Northerners, not truly prejudiced against those of African descent. To the contrary, he did much to help blacks before and during the War, while working hard to heal the rift between the races afterward.

Postwar Forrest, for instance, publicly supported negro suffrage and the last two Civil War Amendments, the Fourteenth and the Fifteenth, saying:

> I advocated the fourteenth and fifteenth amendments before the people, and told our people [that is, white Tennesseans] that they were inevitable and should be accepted.[35]

These black servants ("slaves" to Yankees) picking cotton on a plantation in Mississippi do not belong to Forrest, or to any other white Southerner. They are the property of a wealthy African-American, just one of the tens of thousands of black slave owners in early America. Our liberal educators have left them out of our history books to prevent you from learning about them.

Nowhere are Forrest's real views on race more evident than in a speech he gave at Memphis, Tennessee, on July 4, 1875. His audience was the Independent Order of Pole Bearers, a sociopolitical group of black Southerners and forerunner of the NAACP. As reported by the unreconstructed Memphis *Daily Avalanche*, July 6, 1875, an African-American woman named Miss Lou Lewis, handed Forrest a bouquet of flowers, "as a token, of reconciliation, an offering of peace and good will." Bowing to the crowd, Forrest said:

Miss Lewis, ladies and gentlemen—I accept these flowers as a token of reconciliation between the white and colored races of the South. I accept them more particularly, since they come from a lady, for if there is any one on God's great earth who loves the ladies, it is myself.

This is a proud day for me. Having occupied the position I have for thirteen years, and being misunderstood by the colored race, I take this occasion to say that I am your friend. I am here as the representative of the Southern people—one that has been more maligned than any other. I assure you that everyman who was in the Confederate army is your friend. We were born on the same soil, breathe the same air, live in the same land, and why should we not be brothers and sisters.

When the war broke out I believed it to be my duty to fight for my country, and I did so. I came here with the jeers and sneers of a few white people, who did not think it right. *I think it is right, and will do all I can to bring about harmony, peace and unity. I want to elevate every man, and to see you take your places in your shops, stores and offices. I don't propose to say anything about politics, but I want you to do as I do—go to the polls and select the best men to vote for. I feel that you are free men, I am a free man, and we can do as we please.*

I came here as a friend, and whenever I can serve any of you I will do so. We have one Union, one flag, one country, therefore let us stand together. Although we differ in color, we should not differ in sentiment.

Many things have been said in regard to myself, and many reports circulated, which may perhaps be believed by some of you, but there are many around me who can contradict them. *I have been many times in the heat of battle—oftener, perhaps, than any within the sound of my voice. Men have come to me to ask for quarter, both black and white, and I have shielded them. Do your duty as citizens, and if any are oppressed, I will be your friend. I thank you for the flowers, and assure you that I am with you in heart and hand.*[36]

Here Forrest calls African-Americans "brothers and sisters," assuring them that he is their friend—as is every former white Confederate soldier.

Around this same time Forrest began campaigning for racial equality, coming up with a method to help revitalize the "prostrate South." Noting that it was not necessary for there to be a battle between people of different colors, he declared:

> Let us all work together. In that way our entire nation will flourish.[37]

As he told the Louisville *Courier-Journal*, in an effort to rebuild Dixie he wanted to repopulate the region with both freedmen and new immigrant blacks from Africa.[38] How different this was from Lincoln who, right up until his death, campaigned incessantly to rid the country of blacks altogether, as one of his own generals (Benjamin F. "the Beast" Butler) later detailed in his memoirs.[39]

Union General Benjamin F. Butler testified that Lincoln met with him just days before his assassination to discuss the possible deportation of blacks to Europe, Latin America, the Caribbean, and particularly Africa, the home of the president's favorite black colony: Liberia. A black colony in Central America was to be named after Lincoln: "Linconia."

But Forrest was cut from a different cloth than the typical Yankee. For example, he often remarked on the warm feelings he felt toward blacks, and even had a plan on how to procure new U.S. laborers, not just from Africa, but also from China.[40]

One last glimpse of the real nonracist Forrest was offered to the world after his death on October 29, 1877. During the ensuing funeral services (wake, march, and burial) at Memphis, Tennessee, over the next few days, some 20,000 individuals attended in order to pay their respects to the beloved Southern hero. Among them were President Jefferson Davis, *along with thousands of grieving African-Americans, comprising one-third of the total mourners.*[41]

According to the Memphis *Appeal*, untold numbers of "negroes" (of all ages) "flocked" to Forrest's funeral, demonstrating not only their fascination with the General, but "genuine sorrow" over the demise of the celebrated military man. On the morning of October 31 alone, over 500 blacks walked solemnly past Forrest's casket, and hundreds more asked or were invited to walk in his funeral procession. From them not a single denigrating word was heard. Only adulation and admiration for Nathan Bedford Forrest, the "true friend of the negro."[42]

How different this was from President Abraham Lincoln's funeral at Springfield, Illinois, on May 4, 1865, *at which African-Americans were banned!*[43]

South-haters have long ignored and suppressed these facts. But that does not make them disappear. It only emphasizes them.

Along with Confederate President Jefferson Davis, thousands of African-Americans attended Forrest's funeral in the Fall of 1877, while hundreds officially walked in his funeral procession. Such facts sharply contradict the Yankee myth that the General was a racist who was universally detested by blacks.

2

FORREST & SLAVERY

TWO OF THE ANTI-SOUTH MOVEMENT'S favorite themes are that the Civil War was over slavery and that Forrest was a vile, cruel, and even violent slave holder his entire life. Concerning the first item, since it is germane to our topic, let us cite the two men who knew most precisely what the War was about: Confederate President Jefferson Davis and Union President Abraham Lincoln.

In 1890 here is what Davis said on the topic:

> The truth remains intact and incontrovertible, that the existence of African servitude was in no wise the cause of the conflict, but only an incident. In the later controversies that arose, however, its effect in operating as a lever upon the passions, prejudices, or sympathies of mankind, was so potent that it has been spread like a thick cloud over the whole horizon of historic truth.[44]

On August 15, 1864, in the midst of his war, Lincoln said very much the same thing:

> My enemies pretend I am now carrying on this war for the

sole purpose of abolition. So long as I am President, it shall be carried on for the sole purpose of restoring the Union."⁴⁵

Now that this particular Yankee myth has been exposed, let us address the second one: that Forrest was a barbaric and sadistic slaver until his death in 1877.

If the American Civil War had been fought over slavery it would have ended on January 1, 1863, when Lincoln issued his Final Emancipation Proclamation. Instead it dragged on for another 2 years and four months. In fact, slavery was not officially abolished in the U.S. until December 6, 1865—eight months *after* both the War and Lincoln's death—with the ratification of the Thirteenth Amendment.

To get at the truth behind Forrest's association with slavery it will be beneficial to briefly examine its background.

The actual beginnings of slavery are unknown. This is because by the time of the invention of writing and record-keeping, slavery was already in existence. It was thus a prehistoric institution whose roots can never been definitively established.⁴⁶

Additionally, there is no known region on earth where slavery has not been practiced. Nearly every people, every society, every culture, every continent, and every religion that has been studied has been found to have once engaged in either slavery or the slave trade or both.⁴⁷ Indeed, slavery was the very foundation of such ancient and civilizations as Africa, China, Mesopotamia, Rome, Greece, and the British Isles. Rather than calling it the "peculiar institution" then, as Yankees and Liberals do, it is far more accurate to describe it as the "universal institution."⁴⁸

It would be a mistake to assume, however, that slavery

began and could have only thrived due to racism. The idea of "race" was nonexistent in ancient times, as can be seen in the Bible: the word does not appear anywhere in the Good Book and, in fact, the entire concept of race (division by skin color) is noticeably absent.

The beginnings of slavery are unknown. It was already flourishing all of over the world among every known race, society, religion, and civilization before the invention of writing and record-keeping. Thus slavery was not the "peculiar institution," as Yankees wrongly call it. It was, and still is, the universal institution.

Instead, biblical peoples categorized one another by their nationality.[49] The word "race" was not even invented until 1580,[50] while the word "racism" was not coined until 1902.[51]

Thus slavery began as a nonracist institution in prehistory, at which time people simply enslaved anyone they came across, without regard to their appearance, place of birth, or skin color.[52] Families even enslaved their own members, as is illustrated in the Old Testament story of Joseph, the son of Jacob and Rachel.[53]

It was not until the 17th and 18th Centuries that racist attitudes began to be used as a justification for slavery. For whites this seems to have come, in part, with the realization that the Bible does not condemn slavery (indeed, in some passages it actually condones and even commands it). More importantly, many early Christians (e.g., Mormons) interpreted the "mark of Cain" in Genesis as the "curse of black skin," which forever doomed all Africans to be the "servants of servants."[54]

Moving into the 19th Century, we find that in 1821, the year of Forrest's birth, slavery was legal in every state across the U.S., as was casually noted in the Constitution.[55] But it was not just whites who owned blacks. There were thousands of black slaveholders in early America, many who owned both black and white slaves.[56] For millennia Indians were once enthusiastic enslavers of their own kind,[57] until the arrival of Europeans and African slavery, after which they enslaved whites and blacks as well.⁵⁸

In Africa herself at the time, 1.5 million Europeans and Americans had recently been reduced to slavery (triggering the bloody Barbary Wars in North Africa).⁵⁹ For thousands of years prior to that Africans had been enslaving one another using the most sadistic and savage forms of human bondage ever recorded. Beginning in the 1400s, Africans became the only group to participate in the transatlantic slave trade from beginning to end.

Not surprisingly, the words "Africa" and "African" are now universally associated with slavery; not because of America's 400-year experiment with it, but because no continent, nation, or people on earth has practiced slavery longer or more ardently than Africa. The institution continues to flourish in Africa to this day, almost unimpeded.⁶⁰

Nowhere on earth has slavery been practiced longer, more earnestly, or more sadistically than in Africa. Domestic African slavery was still thriving and expanding well past the Medieval Era, with African kings enslaving and brutalizing millions of fellow Africans. By the late 1700s and early 1800s some 1.5 million whites had been enslaved in Africa as well, sparking the Barbary Wars.

Yankee writers would have you believe that the *American slave trade* was a Southern invention. The truth is that it had nothing to do with the South. This commercial business got its start in Massachusetts in 1638.⁶¹ You have also been deceived into believing that *American slavery* was born in Dixie. But again, there is no connection, for this institution also began in Massachusetts, in this case in 1641.⁶²

The Northeast was, in fact, the slavery capital of the American colonies, and later of the United States,⁶³ from the inception of the institution here in 1638 to December 1865, when human bondage was finally officially outlawed by the Thirteenth Amendment (the Emancipation Proclamation was a fake and freed not a single slave North or South). New York practiced slavery for 239 years, far longer than any other state, making what I call the "Slave Regime State" America's only true slavocracy.[64]

Such facts of history could be multiplied almost indefinitely, and, in order to set the record aright, I have discussed these and many others in detail in my other works.[65]

Despite these facts, or perhaps because of them, the anti-South movement long ago began pronouncing the Old South a "bastion of slavery" and the Confederacy a nation of "evil racist slave owners," to take the focus off itself and its many crimes against the American people and the Constitution.[66]

The man that South-haters put at the top of the "evil racist slave owners" list is Confederate General Nathan Bedford Forrest!

We have already proven that he was not a racist in the traditional sense, and that he was certainly nowhere near as prejudicial as Lincoln and most other Northerners. Now let us look at the actual facts about the General as a slave owner and trader.

Anti-South writers disingenuously promote the idea that slavery was illegal in the 1800s, and that therefore slave-owning Forrest was a criminal. Actually, under the Constitution slavery was legal in every state both North and South at the time. Forrest was not a criminal because he owned slaves.

Pro-North historians tell us that Forrest was a racist because he owned slaves. If this is true, then the millions of Northerners, like Ulysses S. Grant, who also owned slaves, must also be considered racists,[67] as would America's thousands of early black and Indian slaveholders. Forrest was not a racist because he owned slaves.

Anti-South writers claim Forrest was a slave trader his entire life. False. The General was only involved in the slave trade for seven short years, from 1852 to 1859, and was a slave owner for only 11 years, from 1852 to 1863. (Again, this is in stark contrast to Yankees like Grant, who bought, leased, kept, and sold slaves for decades, and only finally emancipated their black chattel when they were forced to under the Thirteenth Amendment.) Recognizing that slavery was coming to an end, Forrest wisely and compassionately closed up his trading company and emancipated his last slaves two years before the start of Lincoln's War (1861), five years before Lincoln's phony and illegal Emancipation Proclamation (1863), and seven years before the Thirteenth Amendment finally officially abolished slavery across the U.S.(1865).[68]

Union General Ulysses S. Grant owned slaves before, during, and after the Civil War, while in the midst of the conflict he declared: "The sole object of this war is to restore the union. Should I be convinced it has any other object, or that the government designs using its soldiers to execute the wishes of the Abolitionists, I pledge to you my honor as a man and a soldier, I would resign my commission and carry my sword to the other side." The fact that Liberals and South-haters call Forrest a racist and not Grant only further exposes their hypocrisy.

What many do not realize is that Forrest got out of the slave trading business in great part because of his slaves themselves. While the North finally abolished its slave trade gradually over a span of many years—and then, only when it became unprofitable—Forrest abolished his immediately and at the height of its profitability in 1859. Why? In large part because his servants had come to him "in a body" with the idea of closing his slave trading business and opening up a plantation, where they could continue to work for him without fear of being sold to someone else.[69]

While Forrest was busy emancipating his African-American servants, here is what Lincoln was saying about slavery, blacks, abolition, and racial equality:

> If all earthly power were given me, I should not know what to do as to the existing institution. *My first impulse would be to free all the slaves, and send them to Liberia [Africa]—to their own native land.* But a moment's reflection would convince me, that whatever of high hope (as I think there is) there may be in this, in the long run, its sudden execution is impossible. If they were all landed there in a day, they would all perish in the next ten days; and there are not surplus shipping and surplus money enough in the world to carry them there in many times ten days. *What then? Free them all, and keep them among us as underlings? Is it quite certain that this betters their condition? I think I would not hold one in slavery at any rate; yet the point is not clear enough to me to denounce people upon. What next? Free them, and make them politically and socially our equals? My own feelings will not admit of this; and if mine would, we well know that those of the great mass of white people will not.*[70]

One of the North's favorite Forrest myths pertains to the manner in which he treated the slaves he sold. According to these fairy tales, Forrest abused and even tortured his slaves, beating many of them to death with chains. As the abuse of slaves was illegal and punishable by fines—and, in extreme cases, even execution—in the South, as only psychopaths engage in the violent mistreatment of others, and since slaves were worth the equivalent of $50,000 a piece in today's currency, this accusation is illogical to say the least. One Yankee newspaper article at the time also claimed that Forrest had two out-of-wedlock children with one of his slave girls, a young black women named Catharine.[71]

As for the former charge, first-hand accounts from those who purchased slaves from Forrest reveal that he was an exemplary master whose slaves were regularly bathed and well-groomed, and daily dressed in clean, freshly starched, stiff clothing. One of Forrest's own slave sale advertisements noted that his rules regarding "cleanliness, neatness and comfort . . . [are] strictly observed and enforced."⁷²

Forrest never had a problem with runaway slaves, one common in the North. Indeed, not only did black Southern servants ask to be purchased by the General, after emancipation nearly all of them enthusiastically came back to work for him.

As for the latter charge, every available piece of evidence shows that Forrest was a faithful husband who remained chaste and loyal to his Christian wife from the day they married in 1845 until the day he died in 1877, 32 years later. The Dixie-loathing journalist who invented this particularly ludicrous story gives himself away by attributing Forrest's "abominable" behavior to the fact that he was born in the "woman-hating, child-thieving South." We Southerners rightly consider this newspaper article a classic piece of anti-South disinformation.⁷³

Along with these obviously fabricated myths we are told that Forrest refused to allow his servants to learn to read and write, that he treated them with contempt, and that he regularly and cruelly divided up his slave families purely for financial gain.

Here is the truth: Forrest encouraged his servants to learn to read and write (quite unlike typical slave treatment in the North), always handled them with respect and dignity, and went out of his way to make sure he did not divide families—even though there was no law against this in Mississippi or Tennessee at the time. Indeed, it was his routine practice to purchase all the members of a slave household if need be, in order to keep husbands, wives, and children together.

In cases where the male heads of slave families had been sold away from their wives and children, Forrest would go in search of them, no matter how widely scattered they happened to be, then purchase them on the spot. Thus in countless instances he was instrumental in reuniting servant families who had been separated. As his biographers Jordan and Pryor write, he was a slaver of "admitted probity and humanity" who never split slave families up, even if he had to take a loss.[74]

Another misconception we must do away with is that Forrest, being a "barbaric slave trader," preferred doing business with the same sort of unsavory individuals. In all actuality, he refused to do trade with inhumane slavers, and, according to journalist Lafcadio Hearn, Forrest possessed a list of especially vicious Memphis slave traders that he refused to sell to.

All in all, Forrest turns out to be the epitome of an honest, genteel, and humanitarian slave trader who made sure that his servants were well housed, well clothed, and well fed, and were sold to reputable, altruistic, kindly owners. Little wonder that Forrest's black servants were "strongly attached to him," or that when he attended slave auctions, blacks would line up and plead for him to buy them.[75]

Confederate Colonel George W. Adair, an intimate friend of the General, summed up Forrest the slave trader this way:

> *Forrest was kind, humane, and extremely considerate of his slaves. He was overwhelmed with applications from a great many of this class, who begged him to purchase them.* He seemed to exercise the same influence over these creatures that in a greater degree he exercised over the soldiers who in later years served him as devotedly as if *there was between them a strong personal attachment.* When a slave was purchased for him his first act was to turn him over to his negro valet, Jerry, with instructions to wash him thoroughly and put clean clothes on him from head to foot. *Forrest applied the rule of cleanliness and neatness to the slaves which he practised for himself.* In his appearance, in those ante-bellum days, he was extremely

neat and scrupulously clean. In fact, so particular was he in regard to his personal appearance that some were almost inclined to call him foppish. *The slaves who were thus transformed were proud of belonging to him. He was always very careful when he purchased a married slave to use every effort to secure also the husband or wife, as the case might be, and unite them, and in handling children he would not permit the separation of a family.*[76]

These are truths about Nathan Bedford Forrest that you will never read in any pro-North book.

Confederate Colonel George W. Adair, founder in 1860 of the daily journal *Southern Confederacy*, was a volunteer aid on Forrest's staff. According to Adair the General was "kind, humane, and extremely considerate of his slaves . . . who were proud of belonging to him," African-American men and women with whom he shared a "strong personal attachment." Yankee myths die hard. But die they must.

3

FORREST & BLACK CONFEDERATE SOLDIERS

IF PRO-NORTH HISTORIANS ARE RIGHT, not a single Southern black supported let alone fought for the Confederacy in Lincoln's War, and Forrest, being a "cowardly and savage racist," took any and every opportunity to brutalize and kill Yankee African-Americans he met on the battlefield. Like all of the other assertions put forth by Northern and New South historians on these topics, however, these too are patent falsehoods. And we will now prove it.

Unlike those who make such statements, I have thoroughly and objectively researched the matter of both black Confederates and Forrest for many decades. While Northerners consider the term an oxymoron, the "black Confederate soldier," or "Old

Confed," as he was endearingly called by whites,[77] was no fiction.

Unofficially an estimated 300,000 Southern black men armed themselves, enlisted, and served heroically under the Rebels' Stars and Bars, 100,000 more than served under the Yanks' Stars and Stripes. This number is even more impressive when we consider that Southern blacks were exempt from the Confederate draft: though many were impressed into service, the rest volunteered.[78]

Additionally, when raw percentages are taken into account, far more blacks fought for the Confederacy than for the Union. The Union possessed about 3 million soldiers. Of these about 200,000 were black, 6 percent of the total. The Confederacy had about 1 million soldiers. Of these an estimated 300,000 were black, 30 percent of the total—24 percent more than fought for Lincoln.

Hundreds of thousands of African-Americans served in one capacity or another in the Confederate army. These two black Confederates, stationed in Alabama, were trained, drilled, uniformed, and armed, serving faithfully for the full duration of the War.

And these numbers are conservative if we use the definition of a "private soldier" as determined by German-American Union General August Valentine Kautz in 1864:

> In the fullest sense, any man in the military service who receives pay, whether sworn in or not, is a soldier, because he is subject to military law. Under this general head, laborers, teamsters, sutlers, chaplains, etc., are soldiers.[79]

Using Kautz's definition of a "private soldier," some 2

million Southerners fought in the Confederacy: 1 million whites and perhaps as many as 1 million blacks. As most of the 4 million blacks (3.5 million servants, 500,000 free) living in the South at the time of Lincoln's War remained loyal to Confederacy, and as at least 500,000 to 1 million of these either worked in or fought in the Rebel army and navy in some capacity, Kautz' definition raises the percentage of Southern blacks who defended the Confederacy as real soldiers to as much as 50 percent of the total Confederate soldier population.[80]

This old illustration clearly shows something that Liberals, scallywags, and pro-North advocates would rather you not ever see: an all-black U.S. infantry being led by a white officer (foreground), part of Lincoln's racist military policies—which called for racially segregated troops and a ban on black officers. In the South, however, whites and blacks, in fact, all of the races, fought side by side in integrated units under President Jefferson Davis' more racially tolerant military program. And unlike in the Union armies, black Confederate soldiers were not required to list their race on their enlistment application.

Using all available records and statistics at our disposal, along with Kautz's statement, it is plain that throughout Lincoln's illegitimate and needless four-year conflict, between 300,000 and 1 million African-Americans served in the Confederate army and navy, many of them as trained and armed soldiers who fought courageously for the South alongside their European-American brethren.[81] This should not be surprising: Dixie was, after all, their homeland as well, and the only one they had ever known. Among these hundreds of thousands of black Confederates were 65 slaves serving under Forrest, 45 of them belonging to the dashing officer himself.[82] Of them the General later said:

> When I entered the army I took forty-seven negroes into the army with me, and forty-five of them were surrendered with me. I said to them at the start: "This fight is against slavery; if we lose it, you will be made free; if we whip the fight, and you stay with me and be good boys [that is, do not try to run away], I will set you free; in either case you will be free." These boys staid with me, drove my teams, and better confederates did not live.[83]

(Let us note here that being a military and political genius, Forrest was perfectly aware that the War was not over slavery. But he also understood that slavery was coming to an end whether the South won or not, and he wanted to give encouragement to his black soldiers—most who had long been looking forward to abolition.)

On another occasion Forrest made these comments about his 45 black Confederate soldiers:

> I said to forty-five colored fellows on my plantation that . . . I was going into the army; that if they would go with me, if we got whipped they would be free anyhow, and that if we succeeded and slavery was perpetuated, if they would act faithfully with me to the end of the war, *I would set them free*. Eighteen months before the war closed I was satisfied that we were going to be defeated, and *I gave these forty-five men, or forty-four of them, their free papers* . . .[84]

Of these 45 African-Americans, Forrest hand-selected seven of them to be his personal armed guards, a service which they proudly provided until he surrendered his cavalry in May 1865.[85]

Throughout the War Forrest routinely used blacks as scouts[86] while energetically pursuing his black impressment and enrollment program,[87] as the following example from his headquarters at Okolona, Mississippi (dated August 5, 1864), reveals. Note that Forrest insinuates that he intends to use these particular blacks, not merely as slave laborers as Lincoln did when he first reluctantly enlisted African-Americans, but as both military workers and regular armed soldiers:

> . . . all that can be done shall be done in North Mississippi to drive the enemy back. At the same time I have not the force to risk a general engagement, and will resort to all other means in my reach to harass, annoy, and force the enemy back. I have ordered the impressment of negroes for the purpose of fortifying positions, blockading roads and fords upon the rivers, and shall strike him [the Yankee] in flank and rear, and oppose him in front to the extent of my ability and fight him at all favorable positions along his line of march.[88]

Forrest enlisted 65 African-American men in his cavalry: 45 of them from his own plantations, 7 of them who served as his personal armed guards. He freed all of them midway through the War. In this Victorian illustration, two of Forrest's soldiers, a black Confederate (front) and a white Confederate (back), reconnoiter a Union encampment in the valley to the right, where a U.S. flag can be seen floating in the breeze above a cluster of Yankee wedge tents.

A comparison between Forrest's wartime treatment of blacks and Lincoln's wartime treatment of blacks will help us get one step closer to the General's real views on this subject.

Contrary to popular belief, Lincoln's approach toward African-Americans was far from what one would expect from the "Great Emancipator." For example, not only did he pay his black soldiers half of what he paid his white soldiers, he also denied his African-American military men pensions, bounties, and bonuses, all which were provided to white Union soldiers. Lincoln even ordered that medical attention be given to whites first. Additionally, rather than issuing freedmen "forty acres and a mule" as he had falsely promised, he decided instead to pen them up like livestock in "government corrals," and withhold food, clothing, and medical care.[89]

On September 26, 1864, at the Brown Farm at Elkton, Tennessee, Forrest came across one of these squalid U.S. black camps and described the situation like this:

> From Elkton I directed my course toward a Government corral at Brown's plantation, toward Pulaski. *At this place I found about 2,000 negroes, consisting mostly of old men, women, and children*, besides a large amount of commissary stores and medical supplies. [Confederate] General [Abe] Buford having completed his work at Elk River joined me at this place, where I issued to my entire command several days' rations, distributing among the troops as much sugar and coffee as they needed. *The negroes were all ragged and dirty, and many seemed in absolute want. I ordered them to remove their clothing and bed clothes from the miserable hovels in which they lived and then burnt up this den of wretchedness. Near 200 houses were consumed.*[90]

We can be sure that Forrest passed these 2,000 African-Americans—the unfortunate victims of Lincoln's "let 'em root, pig, or perish" emancipation policy[91]—into the care of local white families, who freely tended to their every need (just as thousands of white Southerners had done with their own servants) until they were able to fend for themselves.

Despite such reports, all of which appear in the U.S. government's official records,[92] the deceptive Yankee historian tells us that Forrest "killed all of the blacks he came across or captured during the War," a preposterous charge by any standard.

More proof that this is false again comes from Forrest's own pen. What follows is a typical Forrest dispatch, demanding the enemy's immediate surrender. This one was issued on September

24, 1864:

> Headquarters Forrest's Cavalry, in the Field, September 24, 1864. Officer Commanding U. S. Forces, Athens, Alabama: I demand an immediate and unconditional surrender of the entire force and all government stores and property at this post. I have a sufficient force to storm and take your works, and if I am forced to do so the responsibility of the consequences must rest with you. Should you, however, accept the terms, all white soldiers shall be treated as prisoners of war and *the negroes returned to their masters*. A reply is requested immediately. Respectfully, N. B. Forrest, Major-General C. S. Army.[93]

Forrest's critics attack him even for this. But as a law-abiding American citizen he was only obeying the Constitution's "Fugitive Slave Law,"[94] which required that runaway slaves be returned to their rightful owners, or face a fine and imprisonment.[95]

A Confederate reunion of the men of General Nathan Bedford Forrest's Escort, about 1890. One of the most dangerous and successful military outfits ever organized, this specialized racially integrated cavalry unit was both respected and feared by Yankee troops. Near the center a woman is holding up a large Confederate Third National Flag with the words "Forrest's Escort" on it. Three of Forrest's 65 black Confederate soldiers are in attendance. No signs of racism here.

More clues of Forrest's true feelings toward blacks come from after the War. When he returned to his Mississippi plantation

After the War black Confederate soldier and chaplain Louis Napoleon Nelson posed for this photo in his reunion uniform and medals. He fought in numerous battles, including Shiloh and Vicksburg, and served under Forrest at Brice's Crossroads. In the late 1800s and early 1900s he attended 39 Confederate reunions, and at his funeral in 1934 his coffin was draped with a Confederate Battle Flag. Private Nelson's grandson, Nelson W. Winbush, wrote the foreword to the author's bestselling book, Everything You Were Taught About the Civil War is Wrong, Ask a Southerner!

"Green Grove," many of his former black servants ("slaves" to Northerners) returned, as did many of those that he had set free before Lincoln's War, each one keen to become an employee of the man they had once called "Marse Bedford." All became loyal and productive postwar workers, bold facts that once again demolish the Yankee myth that he was a sadistic racist.[96] The story of Thomas ("Tom") Edwards, one of Forrest's black employees, is revealing here.

When the General tried to prevent Edwards from beating his wife, the man turned on him with an axe. An unarmed Forrest wrenched the weapon from his attacker and killed him with it. The next day a *black* judge examined the case and found that the General had acted in self-defense, all charges were dropped, after which he was applauded by his other *black* employees for having rid the plantation of a mean, cruel, violent, temperamental, and dangerous individual.[97]

Another indication of the way Forrest was seen by blacks—in complete opposition to the anti-Forrest propaganda of

Yankee mythology—was that around this time he offered to let his 200 black employees (all former slaves) out of their work contracts. Only eighteen opted to leave. The other 182 chose to stay on.[98]

This photograph destroys two Yankee fictions simultaneously: 1) that Southern whites and blacks detested one another, and 2) that there was no such thing as a black Confederate soldier. Andrew Martin Chandler (left) and one of his family's servants, Silas Chandler (right), are shown here in official Confederate uniforms, full fledged soldiers in the 44th Mississippi Infantry. Armed to the teeth in preparation for the fight against the illicit Northern invaders, such brave young men, white and black, were prepared to face death side-by-side if need be. This type of interracial pairing was repeated hundreds of thousands of times across the South, including in Forrest's cavalry. But you are not supposed to know that.

Yankee agents took notice. One, Union General Oliver O. Howard, commissioner of the Freedmen's Bureau, met with Forrest. After examining his plantation's working conditions Howard noted that the former Rebel officer was doing all that he could to be just and equitable in the handling of his African-American employees. Another, Captain Collis of Connecticut, visited Green Grove and happily reported that General Forrest's management of his farm and black workers was "the best he had ever seen," particularly concerning work hours, free time, and overall quality of life.

Yet curiously, Collis, representing the U.S. government—the same body that had attacked Forrest for "racism" during the War—was also harshly critical of the General for his *leniency* toward his freed black workers. For one thing, the Yankee government did not approve of Forrest's habit of allowing them to carry guns and knives, both during work and at home.

Black Confederate soldier "Uncle" Jerry Perkins served with the Thirty-first Tennessee Infantry. After the War he attended "all of the Confederate Reunions" and was considered a "favorite" among the unit's white Rebel soldiers.

Northern military men also expressed grim dissatisfaction when they learned that he was making generous financial advances to his black employees. It was for granting these "injurious indulgences" that the U.S. government eventually ordered Forrest to cease and desist, with the veiled threat of severe repercussions if ignored. Despite this overt racism from the North, and Forrest's obvious utter lack of prejudice, it is the latter who is routinely pilloried for being a "racial bigot."[99]

Once again, Forrest's own words reveal the truth about his views of African-Americans.

Outrageously, after the War William G. Brownlow, the South-hating Radical Liberal governor of Tennessee at the time, promised that all Southern men who resisted Reconstruction would be tracked down and killed. A reporter asked Forrest about Brownlow's decision to call out his militia against the honorable citizens of Tennessee. Would he respond?

> Yes, sir; if they attempt to carry out Governor Brownlow's proclamation, by shooting down Ku-Klux—for he calls all Southern men Ku-Klux—if they go to hunting down and shooting these men, there will be war, and a bloodier one than we have ever witnessed. I have told these [anti-South Liberal] radicals here what they might expect in such an event. *I have no powder to burn killing negroes. I intend to kill the radicals [that is, white liberals].* I have told them this and more. There is not a radical [Liberal] leader in this town but is a marked man; and if a trouble should break out, not one of them would be left alive. I have told them that *they were trying to create a disturbance and then slip out and leave the consequences to fall upon the negro*; but they can't do it. Their houses are picketed, and when the fight comes not one of them would ever get out of this town alive. We don't intend they shall ever get out of the country. But I want it distinctly understood that I am opposed to any war, and will only fight in self defense. If the militia attack us, we will resist to the last; and, if necessary, I think I could raise 40,000 men in five days ready for the field.[100]

During his interrogation by a U.S. committee after the War Forrest was asked if he had ever opposed giving blacks the right to vote:

> No, sir. My views in regard to this war are probably different from those of most men. I looked upon it as a war upon slavery when it broke out; I so considered it. [Forrest knew this was not true, but said it only to placate his Yankee inquisitors.] *I said to forty-five colored fellows on my plantation that it was a war upon slavery, and that I was going into the army; that if they would go with me, if we got whipped they would be free anyhow, and that if we succeeded and slavery was*

perpetuated, if they would act faithfully with me to the end of the war, I would set them free. Eighteen months before the war closed I was satisfied that we were going to be defeated, and I gave these forty-five men, or forty-four men of them, their free papers, for fear I might be killed.[101]

If Forrest was truly a racist and a cruel slaver, one must wonder why 45 of his slaves proudly fought by his side for four long years, why seven of them willingly and enthusiastically served as his personal bodyguards (surely one of the world's most dangerous jobs), and why so many of these same men had originally lined up eagerly asking to be purchased by him at the slave markets.

A typical U.S. "government corral," where Lincoln sent refugeed and captured blacks during the War. Such camps were usually unfit for livestock let alone humans, and were filled with disease, crime, and the stench of death. In 1864 Forrest encountered one of these prison-like "dens of wretchedness," as he referred to them, in Elkton, Tennessee, where he emancipated nearly 2,000 miserable blacks.

One is also entitled to ask why, if the General (and his white soldiers) detested African-Americans, after the War his black veterans attended dozens of Confederate reunions, where they were welcomed with open arms and showered with honors and medals? Why indeed!

Confederate Captain D. Augustus Dickert spoke for the entire South, including Forrest, when he said of white and black Confederate soldiers—the latter group which had a well-known hatred for Yankees and a justifiable fear of capture by Union troops:

There was a mutual feeling of kindness and honesty between the two. If all the noble, generous and loyal acts of the negroes of the [Confederate] army could be recorded, it would fill no insignificant volume.[102]

4

FORREST & THE BATTLE OF FORT PILLOW

AT THE BATTLE OF FORT Pillow, Henning, Tennessee, April 12, 1864, Confederate General Nathan Bedford Forrest achieved one of his most stunning triumphs. Sadly, in the ongoing effort to malign his good name, obscure the Confederate victory, and maintain support for Lincoln's illegal assault on the South, Yankee mythographers quickly invented the story that a "racist massacre" had taken place; that Forrest and his men had purposefully, and with malice aforethought, killed black Union soldiers as they were surrendering.

Within days the tale had taken on a life of its own, each storyteller adding his own lurid details and embellishments of incidents that never occurred in real life; only in the minds of their inventors.

For example, Forrest and his troops were said to have shot down women and children in the fort, and to have burned black U.S. soldiers alive in their tents, buried wounded blacks alive, and even nailed several of them to floors or the sides of buildings.

We have already proven that neither Forrest or his white soldiers were racists: of his 5,000 soldiers in 1864, at least 65 were black, 45 of them from his own plantations,[103] all of whom were with him during the fight at Fort Pillow.[104] Additionally, as we have seen, the General himself had hand-picked seven from among these African-Americans to be his personal armed guards.[105] And while Lincoln's black soldiers were segregated, Forrest's (like the rest of the Confederate army) were racially integrated—just another illustration of the massive difference in racial attitudes between South and North.[106]

Confederate troops (back) charge Fort Pillow in an attempt to rid the garrison of its "nest" of rogue Union soldiers, galvanized Yanks, vicious criminals, and treasonous scallywags, all which had long been preying on the defenseless men, women, and children in the area. Many of the black Union soldiers in the fort were drunk at the time of the Confederate attack. Boldly refusing to surrender, a large percentage of them died unnecessarily as a result.

Thus the tall tale of the bigoted "Butcher of Fort Pillow" is just that. For those who require more evidence, here it is.

Countering the overt nonsense being put out by the Northern propaganda machine were the bonafide reports of Confederate soldiers who were actually present at the Battle of Fort Pillow. Among them was Sergeant Richard R. Hancock of Company C, Second Tennessee Cavalry. In 1887 Hancock cited the book *The Campaigns of General Nathan Bedford Forrest*: after Forrest's troops withdrew from the area, there remained at Fort Pillow none save the [Confederate] dead who had fallen in storming it, and the [Union] dead of the late garrison, victims, not of unlawful acts of war, as has been so virulently alleged and generally believed at the North, but of an insensate endeavor, as foolishly resolved as feebly executed, to hold a position naturally untenable and badly fortified; victims, we may add, of the imbecility and grievous mismanagement of those weak, incapable officers whom the fortunes of war unhappily had placed over them.[107]

Despite the many authentic testimonies of eyewitnesses like Hancock, nothing could stop the Yankee propagandists once they got started. Even Union President Abraham Lincoln got in on the act of whitewashing authentic history. When his Yankee constituency began demanding retribution for Forrest's alleged crimes at the fort, the Northern chief executive felt compelled to respond. On April 18, 1864, he made the following public remarks at Baltimore, Maryland, promising retaliation if the scuttlebutt turned out to be true:

> A painful rumor—true, I fear—has reached us of the massacre by the rebel forces at Fort Pillow, in the west end of Tennessee, on the Mississippi River, of some three hundred colored soldiers and white officers, who had just been overpowered by their assailants.
> . . . We do not to-day know that a colored soldier, or white officer commanding colored soldiers, has been massacred by the rebels when made a prisoner. We fear it,—believe it, I may say,—but we do not know it. To take the life of one of their prisoners on the assumption that they murder ours, when it is short of certainty that they do murder ours, might be too serious, too cruel, a mistake. We are having the Fort Pillow affair thoroughly investigated; and such investigation will probably show conclusively how the truth is. If after all that has been said it shall turn out that there has been no massacre at Fort Pillow, it will be almost safe to say there has been none, and will be none, elsewhere.

If there has been the massacre of three hundred there, or even the tenth part of three hundred, it will be conclusively proved; and being so proved, the retribution shall as surely come. It will be matter of grave consideration in what exact course to apply the retribution; but in the supposed case it must come.[108]

Lincoln need not have worried himself or his officers, for there were no black Yankees killed during "the surrender" because *no Union soldier, black or white, ever surrendered during the conflict*. Why? Because humanitarian Forrest had promised that if they did, *all* of the Union soldiers, both white and black, would be treated as "prisoners of war."[109] Wanting to avoid imprisonment they fought on. Here is his dispatch from the field to Union Major Lionel F. Booth:

HEADQUARTERS CONFEDERATE CAVALRY, NEAR FORT PILLOW. April 12, 1864.
Major Booth, Commanding U. S. Forces, Fort Pillow:
    MAJOR: The conduct of the officers and men garrisoning Fort Pillow has been such as to entitle them to being treated as prisoners of war. *I demand the unconditional surrender of the entire garrison, promising that you shall be treated as prisoners of war*. My men have just received a fresh supply of ammunition, and from their present position can easily assault and capture the fort. Should my demand be refused, I cannot be responsible for the fate of your command.
    Respectfully, N. B. FORREST, Major-General, Commanding.[110]

What we have here is proof of Forrest's good and humane intentions at the very start of the conflict. No acts of cruelty were premeditated or committed. Just a simple and direct plan to capture the garrison as quickly as possible, with the least amount of fanfare and bloodshed possible, all without a vestige of racism. This was the "Forrest method" after all.¹¹¹

Indeed, for the rest of their lives the General and his men would testify under oath that no atrocities, racist or otherwise, had occurred and that

> all allegations to the contrary are mere malicious inventions, started, nurtured, and accredited at a time, and through a sentiment of strong sectional animosity.¹¹²

Anything else, they repeatedly asserted, was the product of "hysteria" and the overwrought imaginations of enemies of the South. Even those Rebels not with Forrest at the battle understood what had happened there: it was the result of the irrational and belligerent behavior of the Yanks at the fort, despite knowing full well that the garrison would soon be stormed, overrun, overpowered, and taken by the Confederates.

In point of fact, the "massacre" legend resulted largely from Northern journalists. As Forrest himself put it to his men:

> They came forth with threats of vengeance towards you and your commander for the bloody victory of Fort Pillow, made a massacre only by dastardly Yankee reporters.¹¹³

Such statements were corroborated by others in the Confederate army. In 1879, Forrest's superior, General Richard Taylor, one of the most respected and fair-minded men of the War on either side, set the record straight. Forrest, wrote Taylor,

> . . . was a tender-hearted, kindly man. The accusations of his enemies that he murdered prisoners at Fort Pillow and elsewhere are *absolutely false*. The prisoners captured on his expedition into Tennessee . . . were negroes, and he carefully looked after their wants himself, though in rapid movement and fighting much of the time. These negroes told me of Mass Forrest's kindness to them.¹¹⁴

Yet the Northern press at the time complained that the number of Union soldiers who died in the conflict, 40 percent, was far above average: of the 557 Yankee soldiers present (295 whites and 262 blacks), 231 were killed (226 were captured and 100 were wounded).

Yet, a 40 percent death rate among the enemy is exactly what one would expect of a fort taken by assault, the type of approach used by Forrest and his men at Fort Pillow. Or to put it another way, as Jordan and Pryor remark: "For a place taken by storm the loss was by no means heavy."

A few of Forrest's sharpshooters picking off Yankees at Fort Pillow in the Spring of 1864.

What is more, throughout the War the mortality rate among black Union soldiers was always (coincidentally) 40 percent higher than for white Union soldiers. This was due in great part to Lincoln's unequal treatment of his black and white soldiers. Black Union soldiers, for instance, were given inferior training, weapons, ammunition, and clothing, and were often used as shock troops, sent into battle first to spare white lives. Thus the 40 percent figure at Fort Pillow should not be held out as a military anomaly. Rather it was the norm among black Union forces.[115]

In 1902 many of Forrest's men were still alive and able to comment on the so-called "slaughter" at Fort Pillow on April 12, 1864. According to their testimony concerning the Yankee death toll and other alleged atrocities that day,

> it was not greater than the circumstances justified; . . . none were killed after they surrendered, . . . and no prisoners were killed or mistreated in or out of the fort that day or the next day.[116]

Forrest himself avowed that no gun was fired and that no Yankee prisoner was injured after the fort was captured. And even if there had been any barbarities committed, on either side, these would have to be largely attributed to *insania belli* (the "insanity of war"), a terrible but inevitable aspect of all violent conflicts.[117]

There is little question that the South won a decisive victory at Fort Pillow, and that a seemingly unusually disproportionate number of Federal soldiers died, many of them African-Americans. The question is why?

The answer that has come down to us today is part fact, part fiction; part emotion, part politics; part Forrest's ingeniousness, part Yankee stupidity. The complete story will never be known. Nonetheless, we do have some clear facts to work with.

To begin with, a number of the Yankee soldiers, in particular many of the blacks, were thoroughly intoxicated on April 12. After the battle countless barrels of whiskey and kegs of beer and ale were found scattered throughout the fort, up and down the works, with tin dippers and cups tied to them for convenience—as Forrest and his officers later testified.

Standing defiantly on the parapets, black U.S. troops taunted, jeered, shouted obscenities, and made obscene gestures at Forrest's men, daring them to attack. In their thoroughly inebriated state they apparently felt immortal and refused to obey Forrest's usual command to "surrender or die." Unaware at the time that the Federals were drunk, and observing their staunch resistance, Forrest gave his usual order to "shoot at everything blue betwixt wind and water until yonder flag comes down." His soldiers rightfully proceeded to unfurl a galling and murderous fire upon them, and dozens fell.[118]

Other Fort Pillow charges against Forrest and his men are just as easily debunked. The women and children in the fort, who Forrest is said to have executed, had been taken away by boat long before the fighting began.[119]

Part of Forrest's cavalry sweeping in on the first line of Union fortifications at Fort Pillow. No "racist massacre" ever took place on April 12, 1864. As objective military scholars and historians have consistently determined and maintained, the death toll was "normal" for a position taken by storm.

The blacks who Forrest and his troops were said to have buried alive were actually just wounded U.S. soldiers who were "playing dead" in the smouldering ruins of the fort to avoid capture. When Forrest's men came along after the battle, they tossed dirt onto the embers to extinguish them, as was the military custom. Later some of these men died and were discovered by U.S. personnel, who assumed they had been "buried alive."[120]

Another serious charge against Forrest is that *during* the battle he and his men purposefully burned wounded black Yanks alive in their tents and cabins. First, the "burning incident" occurred on April 13, the day *after* the battle, long after all of the Confederate forces had evacuated. Forrest himself had left on the 12th around 6:00 PM and never returned. Second, no Union soldiers could have been burned alive because all of the Federal wounded had been carried out by then.

The exact series of events were as follows.

On the morning of the 13th, Forrest sent a detail back to the fort under his aide-de-camp Major Charles W. Anderson, to bury the "overlooked dead" and collect any remaining weapons. A

Union gunboat, the *Silver Cloud*, then appeared on the scene and began to fire upon the men. As there was no longer any reason to guard the fort, and as they were now under attack by a Yankee gunboat on the river, Anderson ordered his men to vacate the area.

As was the military custom in these situations, upon retreat the enemy's remaining tents and cabins were set ablaze to prevent their contents from being recaptured by the Federals, who were already returning to defend what was left of the fort. The Rebs had no way of knowing this, but there were several dead black soldiers inside the structures, killed during the conflict the day before. Yanks who later came on the scene jumped to the wrong conclusion. It was this inaccurate assumption that gave rise to the patently false rumor that "Forrest had burned black soldiers alive in their tents." As just noted, having left the scene of the battle the night before, Forrest himself was miles away at the time.[121]

Forrest's harshest critics claim that he and his men nailed black and white Union soldiers to wooden beams and tortured them to death. In one case it was alleged that the General pinioned a Yank, Lieutenant J. C. Akerstrom, to the side of a house by his clothing and lit him on fire, burning him alive.

Yet, Union testimony itself contradicted these accusations. In the case of Akerstrom, for example, Federal Private John F. Ray later testified that the lieutenant had been killed during the battle, falling dead right in front of him.

In short, this charge is so patently absurd it scarcely deserves mention. It is false for the same reasons all of the other accusations against Forrest and his men in this chapter are false.[122]

As time passed, Yankee newspapers distorted, exaggerated, and even concocted various events pertaining to Fort Pillow. Why? The usual reason for 19th-Century Yankee yellow journalism: it was another attempt to justify Lincoln's illegal invasion of the South and the Northern hatred of her citizens. Fort Pillow thus became the usual "atrocity story," bloodied up for Northern consumption.

Since the tale of the "massacre" was particularly distasteful to freed slaves, Lincoln and his administration naturally made the most of the trumped-up stories (inciting more discord, racism, and violence), all of which have been handed down to us today as "fact."

Yankee General William T. Sherman—who once said that the Union should do whatever was necessary to kill "that devil Forrest," even if it meant "bankrupting the entire U.S. Treasury"—was asked by Grant to drive Forrest out of West Tennessee, and to prepare for a "prompt retaliation if our men have been murdered after capture" at Fort Pillow. Lincoln and his Secretary of War Edwin M. Stanton also promised to avenge the "massacre"—if the rumor was accurate. Revealingly, however, no one ever followed up on the Union pledge to hunt down Forrest, for not a single piece of hard evidence of the alleged "massacre" ever surfaced. Years later Sherman sided with Forrest, saying that he had spoken to hundreds of his soldiers who had been captured by the great Confederate Chieftain, and all said that he had treated them "very kindly."

But the truth has risen to the surface, despite the North's ongoing attempts to suppress it: later, during the Fort Pillow tribunal, most of the affidavits attesting to Forrest's "butchery" at the battle, in fact, came from black Yankees who were illiterate and could not even sign their own names. As such, the resultant documents were "conflicting and extravagant." Why? Who wrote out this ridiculous paperwork?

Obviously the incriminating "evidence" was illegally penciled in by South-hating Northern whites who had but one intention: to permanently disgrace Forrest and taint his name.

There is also the fact that at least 23 percent (eighteen out of seventy-eight) of those who testified against Forrest were not eyewitnesses, yet their statements were treated with the same solemnity as those who were actually at the scene. Here we have proof that the U.S. government, which revealingly called its final report on the "massacre" a "war measure," tried to create a case against Forrest out of nothing for the sole purpose of tarnishing his reputation and defaming the South. Neither Forrest or any of his subordinates ever ordered a massacre, or even anything illegal. In short, the Union report was anti-South wartime propaganda, pure and simple.[123]

In Washington, D.C., when Lincoln heard about Forrest's "massacre," he immediately sent word to his Secretary of War, Edwin M. Stanton, to investigate "the alleged butchery of our troops." Stanton then contacted Grant in the field, passing on Lincoln's edict, which ordered physical reprisal against Forrest and his offending officers—if found guilty.[124]

Grant bitterly denounced the affair, writing furiously to Sherman on April 15:

> CULPEPER, VA., April 15, 1864—8 p. m.
> Major-General SHERMAN:
>
> Forrest must be driven out, but with a proper commander in West Tennessee there is force enough now. Your preparations for the coming campaign must go on, but if it is necessary to detach a portion of the troops intended for it, detach them and make your campaign with that much fewer men.
>
> Relieve Maj. Gen. S. A. Hurlbut. I can send General Washburn, a sober and energetic officer, to take his place. I can also send you General L. C. Hunt to command District of Columbus. Shall I send Washburn? Does General Hurlbut think if he moves a part of his force after the only enemy within 200 miles of him that the post will run off with the balance of his force?
>
> If our men have been murdered after capture, retaliation must be resorted to promptly.
> U. S. GRANT, Lieutenant-General.[125]

Grant's last sentence clearly illustrates that at the time not even the highest ranking Yankee officers believed that a massacre had taken place, or that Forrest was capable of such an act.[126]

Most revealingly of this fact, however, is that no retaliation against Forrest ever followed, not by Lincoln, Stanton, Grant, or Sherman, or anyone else for that matter. And, as they had all well demonstrated throughout the War, these were not men to shrink from exacting retribution on those they deemed worthy.

Lincoln wanted Forrest apprehended and executed if "the alleged butchery of our troops" at Fort Pillow proved true. But it proved untrue, and Lincoln called off his plot to exact revenge on the innocent General—proving once and for all that there was no "racist massacre" at Henning, Tennessee, that day.

While in the South Lincoln's refusal to avenge Fort Pillow was rightly seen as a further sign of Forrest's innocence, in the North it was taken as just another indication of the president's white supremacist sentiments.[127] Yet years later, in his memoirs, Sherman sided with Forrest, theorizing (correctly) that Forrest would never have led such a murderous assault as the alleged "massacre" ascribed to him, and was instead no doubt out of both eyesight and earshot at the rear. Wrote Sherman:

> . . . I am told that Forrest personally disclaims any active participation in the assault, and that he stopped the firing as soon as he could. I also take it for granted that Forrest did not lead the assault in person, and consequently that he was

to the rear, out of sight if not of hearing at the time, and *I was told by hundreds of our men, who were at various times prisoners in Forrest's possession, that he was usually very kind to them.*[128]

Indeed, it was the testimony of both Confederate and Union eyewitnesses on the stand before the U.S. government's investigative committee that later proved Forrest's innocence. One from the latter category, Union Dr. Charles Fitch, said that he had always believed that Forrest never knew anything about any kind of "massacre."[129]

It was more than obvious, even to many Northerners at the time, that the charges against Forrest were absurd, false, and villainous. Despite leading questions, ignorant "eyewitnesses," and a fully biased court, eventually honest and trustworthy soldiers (from both sides) who were actually at the scene attested to Forrest's innocence, and the U.S. government took him off their list of suspects. In the end, not one of the five charges of the committee's report could withstand a detailed examination of the facts.

For the benefit of history, two of the Yankees who attested to Forrest's innocence deserve special mention. Unsurprisingly, *both were African-Americans.*

The first, a black Union private named Ellis Falls, said that without a doubt Forrest had commanded his men to "stop fighting" when it seemed things were about to get out of control.[130] The second, a black Union private named Major Williams, heard a Confederate yell out during the battle that Forrest did *not* want any blacks killed; that they were to be captured and returned to their owners.[131]

Of course, one thing that none of the Northern papers reported was that the white and black Union troops stationed at Fort Pillow were *segregated*, while Forrest's white and black soldiers at the scene were *integrated*, for segregation of troops was a type of racism unheard of in the Confederate Army, where black and whites fought together, side by side.[132]

66 NATHAN BEDFORD FORREST & AFRICAN-AMERICANS

A photo of a section of the famous Confederate Memorial at Arlington National Cemetery that has been banished from our mainstream history books. Why? Because it shows an armed black Confederate soldier (center) proudly marching off to war, side by side with his white Southern brothers. Proof in stone of the African-American Confederate!

5

FORREST & THE KU KLUX KLAN

WITHOUT QUESTION FORREST IS BEST known among South-haters as "the founder and leader of the Ku Klux Klan." Since they believe he was the archetypal "racist Southern redneck," this is only natural to them. But as it turns out, just as he was not a racist or a "butcher," he was also neither the creator nor the Grand Wizard of the KKK, as we will now see in the following brief review of the documented facts.

To begin with, the New or modern nationwide KKK that was founded in 1915 by William J. Simmons has no relation whatsoever to what I call the "Reconstruction KKK" of the 1860s, despite Simmons' claim that it is "the genuine and original Klan." Indeed, as even members of the modern KKK acknowledge, they are so completely dissimilar in every way that if the modern KKK had not borrowed the name and regalia of the Reconstruction KKK, no informed individual today would make any connection between the two. Why? Because as one former member said in the 1922, they are completely "different in conception, organization and purpose."[133]

The modern KKK, shown here on parade in Washington, D.C. in 1925, was founded in 1915 by William J. Simmons, and has absolutely no connection whatsoever—other than the name and some of the groups' regalia—to what the author calls the "Reconstruction KKK," with which Forrest was loosely associated, and which only lasted from late 1865 to early 1869. Note in the photo above that the official banner of today's KKK is not the Confederate Battle Flag, but the U.S. Flag. The former, in fact, was never used as an emblem by the Reconstruction KKK, and its use by the modern KKK is due to the same ignorance of genuine history possessed by Liberals, both groups who inaccurately continue to regard the Confederate Flag as a symbol of "white supremacy." But Forrest was not a white supremacist and neither were the members of the Reconstruction Klan, nor were the Confederate soldiers who fought beneath its beautiful starry cross.

For example, in 1915 the New KKK banned Jews, Catholics, and foreigners. The original Reconstruction KKK, however, did not exclude anyone, and, in fact, according to the testimony of former constituents, it included Jewish, Catholic, and foreign members. Two of the other many differences were that the Reconstruction KKK did not solicit members or charge a fee to join, while the New KKK did both.¹³⁴

James R. Crowe, one of the founders of the Reconstruction Ku Klux Klan on Christmas Eve, 1865, at Pulaski, Tennessee.

Their missions were completely different as well. The Reconstruction KKK was *not* an anti-black organization, as the Liberal anti-South movement preaches. It was an anti-carpetbag, anti-scallywag organization, designed to maintain law and order while thwarting the efforts of Yankees and pro-North Southerners who were trying to obliterate "Southernness" and Northernize Dixie after the War.¹³⁵ This was, after all, Lincoln's stated intention. In 1862, for instance, he told Interior Department official T. J. Barnett that he planned to change the character of the War to one of "subjugation." "The South," Lincoln told his startled listener, "is to be destroyed and replaced with new propositions and ideas."¹³⁶ Northernization!

The Reconstruction KKK had a second and equally important purpose: to assist Southern refugees, war widows, orphans, and Confederate veterans, whatever their skin color. Thus it also served as a Southern relief-and-aid society. The Reconstruction KKK became, in other words, "the salvation of the South," for it was founded on the "sacred principles" of the "love and protection of home." A former Reconstruction KKK member put it like this:

> We were law-abiding citizens, and were organized only for the protection of our women, children, and homes, and to enforce the law and insist on its enforcement.¹³⁷

Forrest himself accurately called the body a "protective, political, military organization," maintaining that it was

> intended as a *defensive organization* to offset the Union

League; to *protect ex-Confederates from extermination* by [Liberal Tennessee Governor William G.] Brownlow's militia; [and] to *prevent the burning of [Southern] gins, mills and residences.*[138]

To get a better understanding of what the Reconstruction KKK was and was not, let us look at the group's Constitution, which laid out its "objects" in plain language:

> *This is an institution of Chivalry, Humanity, Mercy, and Patriotism:* embodying in its genius and principles all that is chivalric in conduct, noble in sentiment, generous in manhood, and patriotic in purpose; its peculiar objects being:
> First—To *protect the weak, the innocent, and the defenseless*, from the indignities, wrongs and outrages, of the lawless, the violent and the brutal, to *relieve the injured and oppressed*, to *succor the suffering and unfortunate*, especially the widows and orphans of Confederate soldiers.
> Second—To *protect and defend the Constitution of the United States*, and all laws passed in conformity thereto, and to protect the States and the people thereof from all invasion from any source whatever.
> Third—*To aid and assist in the execution of all constitutional laws*, and to protect the people from, unlawful seizure, and from trial except by their peers in conformity to the laws of the land.[139]

The matter of the purposes of the Reconstruction KKK being permanently settled, let us now address the question of who founded it.

Because it was created in 1865, Forrest could not have been the originator, for he was not even introduced to the organization until late 1866 or early 1867, one to two years after its formation. The founders' names, in fact, are well-known, as is the exact date of its creation: it was established by six men in Pulaski, Tennessee, on Christmas Eve, 1865—at which time Forrest was living and working in Memphis. The names of these six men were Captain John C. Lester, Captain John B. Kennedy, Captain James R.

Crowe, Richard R. Reed, Frank O. McCord, and J. Calvin Jones.[140]

While Forrest later became an ardent supporter of the KKK, there is no hard evidence that he was the Grand Wizard, or even a member. It is most probable that George Washington Gordon (the man who some say introduced Forrest to the KKK) was Grand Wizard during the short life of the Reconstruction KKK, as Gordon's own wife, Ora Susan Paine, later testified.[141] All other assertions and theories are fantasies, without "factual or logical foundation."[142]

The author's cousin former Confederate General George Washington Gordon, not Forrest, was the one and only true Grand Wizard of the Reconstruction KKK.

Claims by a few KKK members and several of the founders that Forrest was the group's Grand Wizard do not stand up to close objective scrutiny. And, in fact, such claims are negated by other Klansmen who said that he was not, as well as by testimony that others (including Gordon) served as the group's first and only Grand Wizard. Not even the U.S. government could find any evidence that Forrest was the leader of the Reconstruction KKK. In the end, there is simply no irrefutable proof for this assertion, and since KKK members never wrote anything down (under penalty of death), this effectively decides the matter of the Reconstruction KKK's founders and its first leader.[143]

The rumors that Forrest was the founder and Grand Wizard of the Reconstruction KKK were started by anti-South advocates shortly after the War in order to disgrace Forrest, his family, and his soldiers. As the order did not keep written records, no one can prove that either of these legends have any truth to them. And in fact, numerous people, including authentic KKK members, testified that they were patently false.

Furthermore, unlike the Liberal North, the Conservative South did not view the KKK as a "pernicious order made up of ruthless ruffians and racists," and so it would not have hurt Forrest's reputation to have been associated with it. In fact, it would have benefitted him in Dixie—which, after the hearsay began to spread, is precisely what happened.[144]

This illustration, from 1868, reveals the true enemy of the Reconstruction KKK: it was not blacks, but *carpetbaggers* (hanging on right), treacherous Northern whites who came South after the War in order to prey on the ravaged region, and *scallywags* (hanging on left), turncoat Southerners brainwashed by Yankee myth and who sided with the Liberal North.

Naturally, the trouble-making uninformed Yankee propagandists who started the rumors about Forrest and the Reconstruction KKK were the same ones who started the rumor that the order was a racist group. This proves that such gossip was both politically motivated and false.[145]

While a small minority of white KKK members were indeed racists (there are always racists of *every* color in *every* organization), as we have seen, the Reconstruction KKK itself was not a racist organization in either "conception, organization or purpose." It was, as Forrest described it, a "defensive and protective" group intended to assist *all* Southerners, whatever their skin color.[146]

This helps explain why many blacks aided, and were even tortured and died for, the Reconstruction KKK in fighting carpetbaggers and scallywags, and it is also why the order had thousands of black members and even an all-black Ku Klux Klan at Nashville.[147]

The truth of the matter is that during the Reconstruction KKK's short life span, Forrest threatened to shoot any whites who harassed blacks. This warning included both white Northerners and white Southerners, and was actually carried out on at least one occasion that we know of.[148]

In early 1869, when Forrest felt the organization had fulfilled its stated purpose (to aid and protect the South and her citizens), he ordered it to be closed down. Then, as S. E. F. Rose put it, having accomplished its great mission "in relieving the South from the galling yoke of Carpet-Bag rule . . . this strange and mysterious order passed out of existence forever." Thus the Reconstruction KKK, which (unlike the modern KKK) was only meant to be temporary, lasted just a little over three years: from late 1865 to early 1869.[149]

As further proof that Forrest was not the bigoted villain the North portrays, he, or perhaps a leader within the KKK, had several Klan members tried and executed for ignoring Forrest's

The man underneath this KKK costume from the Reconstruction period was not a European-American. He was an African-American who belonged to the all-black Ku Klux Klan den in Nashville, Tennessee. No Liberal will ever speak about this group, or of the thousands of Southern blacks who supported, assisted, and rode with the Reconstruction KKK during its short three-year life span.

order to dissolve the group.¹⁵⁰

Forrest was neither the founder or the leader of the Reconstruction Ku Klux Klan. According to him he was not even a member, though he said he supported the organization. At most, as Tennessee's most influential former Confederate officer at the time, he seems to have been some kind of adviser—but even this is not known for sure since the group never recorded anything on paper. Even if Forrest was the Grand Wizard this would not tarnish his noble character or harm his sterling reputation. For the Reconstruction Klan was a *nonracist* body whose sole function was to protect *all* Southerners from the damage and crimes of Yankee Reconstruction, 1865 to 1877.

Later, in 1871, Forrest was questioned before a U.S. government committee investigating the Reconstruction KKK, where he was found innocent of any misconduct associated with the organization. This fact alone should end any and all disputes concerning Forrest and his relationship with the Reconstruction Klan.¹⁵¹

The overt hypocrisy of those who denounce both Forrest and the Reconstruction KKK is evident from a single fact: not only do they never condemn modern *black* racist organizations, in many cases they actually condone and embrace them. The U.S. tax-payer funded Public Broadcasting System (PBS), for example, continually lambasts both the Reconstruction KKK and the New KKK, yet it supported, funded, distributed, and aired a documentary put out by the Black Panthers in September 2015.¹⁵²

Even if Forrest had been a KKK member, the Grand Dragon of Tennessee, or even the Grand Wizard of the entire organization, it would not diminish his reputation here in the traditional South. This is because the Reconstruction Klan, being merely a *temporary* social aid and protection society, was not something that any educated person would be ashamed of. To the contrary, millions of knowledgeable Southerners (and many non-Southerners) continue to celebrate the original Reconstruction KKK as a venerable and honorable organization that helped "save the South" during the outrages and crimes of the North's "Second Civil War" on Dixie: the grossly misnamed era of so-called "Reconstruction."[153]

John Booker Kennedy, another one of the six original founders of the Reconstruction KKK in 1865.

Whatever Forrest's exact relationship with the Reconstruction KKK, the order itself was an understandable and entirely justifiable expression of Southern pride, esteem, and survival considering the dreadful circumstances imposed on it by the vindictive Liberal North during the postwar era. In 1921 Winfield Jones, a Copperhead, wrote that the

> *Ku Klux Klan was only a manifestation of the spirit of opposition to reconstruction measures taken by the North, and the masked rider in his white robe was a symbol of the spirit of the South in revolt against carpetbag government and negro misrule. These are facts that cannot be explained away, and today our Northern historians, no matter how unpalatable the facts, recognize that conditions existing in the South in reconstruction times were intolerable. . . .* As the South had been defeated on the battlefields and was absolutely bankrupt after Appomattox, the Southern people were not in a position to start another armed rebellion. But the organization of *the Ku Klux Klan undoubtedly was a form of rebellion against the tyranny of reconstruction policies.*

> The American Colonies revolted from Great Britain in 1776, under provocations that were not nearly as irksome and irritating as the conditions which were imposed on the South during reconstruction.[154]

Dixie rests easy in these historical facts just as they stand, and will never cease honoring our great Confederate chieftain, General Nathan Bedford Forrest. We will also continue to memorialize those who served in the Reconstruction KKK in order to save the Southern people from the vitriolic attempts of the Lincoln and Grant administrations to reconstruct them in the North's image after the War.

Forrest would certainly have concurred with one of the KKK's founders, John B. Kennedy, who in 1914 wrote:

> The Ku Klux Klans were composed of the very best citizens of our country; their mission was to protect the weak and oppressed during the dark days of Reconstruction. To protect the women of the South, who were the loveliest, most noble and best women in the world. The survivors are old men now, old with their memories of other days long past, to cheer them during life's twilight. They are proud they were Ku Klux, and could give aid to these dear Southern women again during the Reconstruction period, for it was a dark and distressing era in our beloved Southland. We did nothing to make us ashamed; our acts were always for the good of our country and those we loved. After the lapse of all these years, the survivors of the Ku Klux Klan are gratified to hear the verdict of many who say to us, "Well done; you undoubtedly saved the beautiful Southland during the Reconstruction era."[155]

Let us turn to Forrest himself as the final arbiter on the Reconstruction KKK and his association with it.

When questioned by the Congressional committee about any murders that might have taken place under the auspices of the KKK, Forrest alluded to the well-known fact across the South that both whites *and* blacks were members of the Klan (as noted, there was even an all-black KKK chapter in Nashville at the time):

> Well, yes, sir; there were men [carpetbaggers] killed in Tennessee and in Mississippi by bands in disguise. There were [KKK] men found down there disguised, *white men and negroes both*.[156]

The original Ku Klux Klan, the Reconstruction KKK, with which Forrest was connected, only resorted to violence as a last resort—and this was seldom necessary. In fact, the use of violence was against its formal policies and Constitution. Its primary weapons were intimidation, threats, and fear, which its members put into effect by wearing bizarre apparel and using otherworldly (mostly meaningless) words and symbols. The purpose? To help "motivate" trouble-making carpetbaggers, scallywags, and Reconstructionists to move out of the area as quickly as possible. The violence and racism so often wrongly associated by the anti-South movement with the Reconstruction KKK came later, and was perpetuated by imposters; men who hid behind the robes and masks of the KKK in order to commit crimes without being identified. These racist outlaws caused considerable problems for the Reconstruction Klan, and were one of the reasons Forrest dissolved the organization in early 1869.

When Forrest was asked if he was trying to suppress the many "outrages" then being committed by a few racist black groups against whites, Forrest said no. I am, he stated clearly and publicly, trying to suppress outrages being committed

> by *all* people; my object was to keep peace.[157]

When Forrest was asked if Southern blacks were "suffering

from the hands of the white men as many wrongs after the war as before and during the war," Forrest replied:

> I think more; I do not think they were suffering any during the war.[158]

When asked if he knew personally of any conflicts between whites and blacks, Forrest said:

> I will mention one case that occurred in 1868. At Crawfordsville, on the Mobile and Ohio Railroad, the citizens and negroes had a difficulty, and the negroes threatened to burn the town. It was telegraphed up to West Point, forty miles above there, and to Columbus also. I was then on my way to Memphis.
> When I got to the Mobile road I found these men had got all the trains they could and started down, and I went with them. The negroes were about eight hundred strong, and were out at the edge of the town; the people of the town had fortified themselves; the negroes had burned one house.
> When I got there I got the white people together, organized them, and made speeches to them. I told them to be quiet, and we would see if this could be settled. I then got on a horse and rode over to the negroes and made a speech to them. The negroes dispersed and went home, and nothing was done; there was nobody hurt, nobody molested.
> But they were just on the point where it was liable that fifty or five hundred men would be killed. Those negroes had fallen out [that is, gotten upset] with a young [white] man who was going down the road; his horse had got scared when they came along, had kicked out a little, and run against their trumpeter and knocked him down. They followed him into town to beat him, and then they gathered together.
> I am satisfied I prevented bloodshed there by getting those men together and talking to them, and by talking to the negroes and getting them to go home.[159]

When asked by a reporter if he thought the original

Reconstruction Ku Klux Klan (as opposed to the modern KKK, with which, as we have seen, it has no connection)[160] was of any benefit to the state of Tennessee, Forrest said:

> No doubt of it. Since its organization, the [Yankee-formed anti-South] leagues have quit killing and murdering our people. There were some foolish young men who put masks on their faces and rode over the country, frightening negroes; but orders have been issued to stop that, and it has ceased. You may say, further, that three members of the Ku-Klux have been court-martialed and shot for violations of the orders not to disturb or molest people.[161]

When Forrest was asked, again, about the purpose of the KKK, he said:

> [It was] for the purpose of preventing crime, and for the purpose of protecting each other in case of sickness, or anything—preventing disorder.[162]

When asked "who" the KKK was supposed to prevent disorder from, Forrest said: "By anybody."[163]

Regarding Forrest, the Klan, and other related matters, Confederate Captain James Harvey Mathes noted the following in his 1902 Forrest biography. In the 1860s, Mathes writes:

> *The passions and prejudices of the war began to die out, and no one hailed the end with more pleasure than General Forrest.* The real Kuklux existed only a year or two, and having accomplished its purpose as far as possible by such means, was disbanded as secretly as it was formed and was heard of no more. That General Forrest was at least an adviser in this movement there is very little doubt, but *he and other good Confederates had nothing to do with the so-called or bogus Kuklux Klans which cropped up from time to time afterward, and are even yet counterfeited under different names.* It is due to General Forrest to say, and it will not be questioned by any fair or intelligent critic of his character, that he was ever true to his parole

after he returned home, as well as to the laws of the State and General Government, and to the old flag. *His courage in battle was fully matched by his intrepidity and sense of honor in all the affairs of life.* From his youth up Forrest seems to have had a respect for religious matters, no doubt owing to the teachings of a pious mother. His wife, whom he fairly adored, was a devout member of the church, and had much influence over him. He often said that he attributed his many marvelous escapes in the war to the prayers of his wife and mother. When in camp he always had the chaplain or other suitable person to say grace at meals, and have prayers at night when practicable.[164]

These words, as well as those of the General himself, speak volumes for those who "have ears to hear."

William Joseph Simmons, founder and Imperial Wizard of the new or modern KKK—known as the Knights of the Ku Klux Klan—in 1915. Though there are no real similarities between his organization and the Reconstruction KKK (aside from the name), he claimed there were, and this myth has been wrongly used by the Left to savage Forrest and the good people of the South ever since.

6

FORREST & AFRICAN-AMERICANS IN SUMMARY

THE ANTI-SOUTH MOVEMENT NEVER TIRES of berating, besmirching, and slandering Nathan Bedford Forrest. Each year dozens of new articles and books appear from uneducated South-haters eviscerating the General for traits he never possessed, for crimes he never committed, and for beliefs he never held.

The ignorance surrounding him is truly appalling. But what more can one expect from a much maligned minority made up of uneducated Liberals, far left radicals, socialists, communists, collectivists, anti-traditionalists, anti-Christians, anti-Southers, and anti-Americans; a thin-skinned, dishonest, easily offended group that hates the First Amendment, fears facts, abhors reality, shuns debate, thrives on wishful thinking and "imaginary philanthropy,"[165] and enjoys rewriting history while imposing censorship on everyone but themselves?

We in the South do not take the lies and insults about Forrest lying down, and it is time for everyone who loves Truth to stand up for not only the General, but for authentic history. Facts are facts. And though the mainstream Liberal media has nothing but disdain for them, they will not go away, and we ourselves will not allow them to be buried beneath a mountain of misinformation, disinformation, and silly and often vicious anti-South propaganda.

The Barbary Wars were triggered by the kidnaping, enslavement, and abuse of some 1.5 million whites by Africans—yet another topic Liberals would like to ban.

The North and the New South have been in control of Southern history for far too long; they have polluted the minds of our children for far too long; and they have turned Americans against one another for far too long. While revising, suppressing, and ignoring true American history is the stock and trade of the anti-South movement, preserving, exposing, and acknowledging it is the stock and trade of the pro-South movement. This book is one result of the latter.

Nothing and no one better epitomizes the falsehoods fabricated by foes of the South than Forrest. Yet we have shown here, in a hundred different ways, that:

☛ Forrest was not a "racist." In fact, he stated repeatedly that he was not the enemy of blacks, but their friend, and held out the offer to aid any black man or woman in need. All they had to do was come to him. Forrest backed up his equalitarianism with action: after Lincoln's War he sought to repopulate and rebuild the devastated South with both freedmen and immigrant blacks from Africa, hiring new African-Americans and rehiring former servants by the hundreds.

☛ Forrest was not a "violent and abusive slaveholder." In fact, he treated his servants with the utmost care and respect, never ill-used them, never split up slave families, and never sold them to cruel slavers. Indeed, he was responsible for reuniting a number of servant families who had been divided by others. And unlike Union General Ulysses S. Grant, he emancipated most of his servants before the War, and the rest during the War.

Misinformed and malevolent enemies of the South like to compare Forrest to Adolf Hitler, but were there really any similarities? Hitler was a socialist dictator who enslaved then tortured and killed untold millions. Forrest was a conservative (the opposite of a socialist) Confederate (the opposite of a dictator) who bought individuals who were already slaves and who had asked to be purchased by him, enlisted them in his army, set them free a few years later, rehired them as free men after the War, then went on to campaign for black civil rights.

☛ Forrest was not "anti-negro" during Lincoln's War, and never once tried to deter blacks from joining the Confederate army. To the contrary, he asked them to join—with the offer of complete and permanent manumission. At least 65 African-Americans that we know of rode, served, and fought with the General, 45 of them from his own plantation system. Of these he chose seven to act as his personal armed guards, illustrating the absolute trust and admiration that existed between he and his African-American soldiers. As he promised, in 1863, midway through the War, he freed all 45 of them. That they stayed with him for the rest of the conflict, risking their lives for the Southern Cause (constitutional self-government), only further reveals the true nature of the General's relationship with his black troops.

Yankee slave traders separating a newly arriving African slave mother from her child. In Dixie the practice of dividing up slave families was a rare occurrence, and in fact in some Southern states, such as Louisiana, it was illegal. Forrest did not need a law to know it was wrong, which is why he not only refused to split up slave homes, but went out of his way to reunite servant families, even if it meant taking a financial loss.

☞ Forrest was not a "sadistic racist butcher" at the Battle of Fort Pillow, and neither were his white soldiers. The 40 percent death rate among the Union troops there was "normal" for a weak position taken by assault. Most of the black Yankee soldiers were drunk during the fight, behaved overconfidently, and suffered the consequences. All of the other so-called "racist crimes" allegedly perpetuated by Forrest and his men at Fort Pillow were the result of accidents, misunderstanding, illusion, and the outright lies of enemies of the South. In fact, a number of black Yankee soldiers at the scene sided with the General, helping to clear his name.

☞ Forrest was neither the founder or leader of the Reconstruction

Ku Klux Klan. And even if he had been, no educated person would count this against him, for the Reconstruction KKK was not a white racist group. It was an anti-carpetbag, anti-scallywag organization that served as both a protective body and an aid-and-relief society; one that, according to Forrest himself, served *all* Southerners, whatever their skin color.

The General's own words support these bold facts, as do the testimonies of countless eyewitnesses who knew him, served with him, and worked for him.

Let us end our examination into the racial views of Nathan Bedford Forrest by reprising a portion of his speech to the Independent Order of Pole Bearers (a group of black Southerners and the forerunner of the modern NAACP) at Memphis, Tennessee, on July 4, 1875:

> This is a proud day for me. . . . being misunderstood by the colored race, I take this occasion to say that I am your friend. I am here as the representative of the Southern people—one that has been more maligned than any other. I assure you that everyman who was in the Confederate army is your friend. We were born on the same soil, breathe the same air, live in the same land, and why should we not be brothers and sisters.
>
> . . . I think it is right, and will do all I can to bring about harmony, peace and unity. I want to elevate every man, and to see you take your places in your shops, stores and offices. . . . I feel that you are free men, I am a free man, and we can do as we please.
>
> I came here as a friend, and whenever I can serve any of you I will do so. We have one Union, one flag, one country, therefore let us stand together. Although we differ in color, we should not differ in sentiment.[166]

After reading such statements (of which he made many), the only excuse for calling Forrest a racist is ignorance or maliciousness, period.

86   NATHAN BEDFORD FORREST & AFRICAN-AMERICANS

Contrary to popular thought, as well as the misguided opinion of Liberals, the South did not engage in the American slave trade. From its birth in 1631 to its death in 1865, it was purely a Yankee enterprise,—founded, operated, and funded by Northern businessmen. The slave ship pictured here, for example, has docked at a slave port in New York, both the capital of the American slave trade and the state which practiced slavery longer than any other: 239 years. This makes early New York a true slave regime and America's only genuine slavocracy.

As for the traditional South, we will continue to hold Nathan Bedford Forrest in the highest esteem. For he embodied all that is good and true about Dixie, the Confederacy, and the Old South. His name, his image, his statues, his monument, and his grave site will always be considered holy to those who are familiar with the real man. Indeed, as I have stated many times throughout my literary works, the more one gets to know Forrest, the more one comes to admire, value, and love him.

He was a unique and fascinating individual who should be honored by everyone, by all races, all creeds, and all nationalities. It is true that like every other European-American living in the Victorian Era, he was encumbered with both the positive and negative values, attitudes, and conventions of his time and place. But we should never use presentism to judge our ancestors, for we do not want our descendants using presentism to judge us 150 years from now!

I have been asked many times: "Why should we honor Forrest today? What relevance does he have in the 21st Century?"

If Nathan Bedford Forrest had never been anything but a rugged individualist, a natural born rebel, and stalwart mountain man who, though he began in poverty, became a self-made multimillionaire by the age of 40, he would still deserve our admiration and respect. But he was far more than an achiever of the American Dream.

The General was a champion of the people, of personal liberty, and of political independence, making him both an emblem of freedom and a great American patriot. And since he fought and nearly died trying to preserve the Constitution, while leaving most of his estate to war widows and orphans, he must be ranked as one of the greatest philanthropists in American history, one that every Conservative and Libertarian should be proud of.

Forrest in 1875, two years prior to his death in Memphis, Tennessee, on October 29, 1877. The famous rough and tumble mountaineer, intrepid cavalry officer, and American patriot rightly continues to be revered by people of all races around the world.

Furthermore, as pertains to the topic of this book, Forrest was not an enemy of the black race, but a comrade; not a divider of the races, but a unifier of the races; not a racist, but a true egalitarian and a humanitarian. He was, as his friends, servants, and soldiers knew him, "a tender-hearted, kindly man" who would go out of his way to assist anyone, whatever their complexion.

And that is how Confederate General Nathan Bedford Forrest will always be remembered by those who love the Truth.

Photo © Lochlainn Seabrook

APPENDIX A

General N. B. Forrest in 1864

BY DR. JOHN A. WYETH OF ALABAMA
AUGUST 1895

In the light of history there stands out in clear relief the figure of Lieutenant-General Nathan Bedford Forrest, the most remarkable man our Civil War developed, and the greatest fighter of which the world has an authentic record. Endowed with a physical frame which resisted fatigue and exposure, a muscular organization developed into athletic proportions by reason of the hard manual labor necessity compelled him to perform from the earliest years of boyhood until he was a man, he possessed that quality of mind which never entertained the fear of personal disaster, nor in the flurry of hand-to-hand combat, nor the excitement or confusion of battle, lost for an instant the calm appreciation of what was transpiring. Quick to perceive in the rapidly shifting scenes of battle the opportunity for a fatal blow, he struck as the lightning flashes, blinding and withering. Before his sudden onslaught, to waver was rout; and in his tireless and unrelenting pursuit, rout became panic.

Without education and absolutely without any knowledge of war gleaned from the study of what others had accomplished, he evolved and put into execution the tactics and the strategy of the most famous generals in history. In his terse phraseology: "The way to whip 'em, is to get there first with the most men," and although his greatest victories were won with forces numerically inferior, he so fought his men that where he struck, he was equal to or stronger than his adversary. He realized the value of boldness even when akin to rashness, and, when possible, he attacked notwithstanding the disparity of numbers. When the enemy was about to charge, or was charging, his rule was to go at them at once. He knew that the excitement of a forward movement inspired even the timid with courage; while to stand in the open to receive the thundering onslaught of a cavalry charge, was a severe test of the courage of the bravest, and demoralizing to the timid. The active defensive was in him an intuition. Moreover, he fought his artillery as if they were shot-guns, charging right up to the opposing lines, their double-shotted contents at short range dealing death and disaster. Although his soldiers were called "mounted infantry" and "Forrest's Cavalry," they were neither infantry nor cavalry. There was not a bayonet in his command, and early in the war the sabre was discarded for the repeating pistol. They fought on horse or foot to suit the conditions.

It is probable that not a regiment he commanded could have made a correct tactical manœuvre on foot in action: and beyond the formation by fours and the evolution into line for the charge, the cavalry manual was practically obsolete. With the men he led, strict discipline was impossible; and yet they fought with the steadiness of trained veterans, under the wonderful influence of one who inspired the timid with courage, and the brave with the spirit of emulation.

He said, "War means fighting, and fighting means killing," and when the enemy were not hunting him, he was hunting for them. Ever in the thickest of the fray, it is a marvel that he lived to see the war end. If ever man had a charmed life, such was his. The missile of the assassin, the gun and sabre of the open and honorable foe, turned from their mortal purpose. He was on over one hundred different occasions under fire, and these include the bloody and hotly contested battles of Fort Donelson, Shiloh, Chickamauga, Franklin, and Nashville. "Twenty-seven horses were shot under him," states Gen. James R. Chalmers; and a famous writer, himself a soldier, (Lieut. Gen. Richard Taylor), says: "I doubt if any commander since the days of lion-hearted Richard has killed so many of his enemies as Forrest." His word of command as he led the charge, was, "Forward, men, and mix with them!" Though torn with bullets, and hacked in countless places with the sabre, or hurled from his horse in death struggle of the melée, his life was spared to serve to the end the cause which no man better served than he.

In a personal note Dr. Wyeth writes that he has for some time been getting up material with a view to writing the life of General Forrest, and adds:

Knowing that there are a good number of soldiers in Tennessee who served under Forrest, and who could give me much valuable information in regard to his wonderful achievements as a soldier, as well as his personal qualities, I have thought that the *Veteran* might be the best means of getting at those who served under him and are still living.

I consider General Forrest the most wonderful man in the history of our Civil War, and am sure everybody in the South and every Confederate soldier should be glad of an opportunity to do something toward perpetuating his marvelous achievements.[167]

Andrew John Duncomb of Seminole, Oklahoma, holding the Confederate Battle Flag. A rancher, horse trainer, and Conservative who describes himself as a "black rebel," Duncomb is no anomaly: he is one of thousands of African-Americans who understand and admire Nathan Bedford Forrest. The organization to which Duncomb belongs, "Oklahoma Confederate Veterans Lives Matter," is dedicated to honoring and preserving the names of the Confederate dead—including, of course, the illustrious Tennessee General, still known endearingly here in the Volunteer State as "Ol' Bedford."

APPENDIX B

General N. B. Forrest & the Battle of Fort Pillow

FROM AN ARTICLE BY ONE WHO WAS THERE

CONFEDERATE MAJOR CHARLES W. ANDERSON, STAFF OFFICER UNDER FORREST
NOVEMBER 1895

The charges against Gen. Forrest and his men of massacre and butchery at Fort Pillow are outrageously unjust and unfounded. He did every thing in his power to induce a surrender and avoid an assault. Thrice was a surrender demanded, and as often refused. There never was any surrender, therefore no massacre after surrender, as has been so erroneously and widely charged.

I take occasion here to say that in my long service with Gen. Forrest, his kindness to the vanquished, the unarmed and unresisting foe, was a marked characteristic of the man. He believed and always said and felt, that "war meant fight, and fight meant to kill," but never in all his career did a Federal soldier throw down his arms and surrender, that did not receive at once his consideration and protection. He captured many thousand Federals [according to the General himself, at least 31,000], and there is not one living to-day who can truthfully say that he was ever mistreated or ever insulted by Nathan Bedford Forrest.[168]

APPENDIX C

General N. B. Forrest Monument at Rome, Georgia

From *Historic Southern Monuments*, 1911

N. B. Forrest Monument, Rome, Georgia, 1908

The N. B. Forrest Monument

The Forrest monument is 25 feet high, with base 10 feet square. The whole structure is of granite except the statue, which is of purest Carrara marble, 6 feet 2 inches high, the exact height of the General.

The symbols of ornamentation on two sides of the pedestal suggest the cavalry arm of the service—short sword and bugle. On the other side, flag with broken staff.

The monument stands on Broad Street, the main business street of Rome.—Mattie B. Sheibley

INSCRIPTIONS ON MONUMENT

Front
C.S.A. (Flag)
1861
ERECTED BY N.B. Forrest Chapter
United Daughters of the Confederacy
May 3rd, 1908
N.B. Forrest

Right
1865
"FORREST'S CAPACITY FOR WAR SEEMED ONLY TO BE LIMITED BY THE OPPORTUNITIES FOR ITS DISPLAY."
—General Beauregard.

"HIS CAVALRY WILL TRAVEL A HUNDRED MILES IN LESS TIME THAN OURS WILL TEN."—General W. T. Sherman.

Left

"HE POSSESSED THAT RARE TACT, UNLEARNABLE FROM BOOKS, WHICH ENABLED HIM, NOT ONLY EFFECTUALLY TO CONTROL HIS MEN, BUT TO ATTACH THEM TO HIM PERSONALLY, 'WITH HOOKS OF STEEL.'"—Wolseley.

Rear

ON SUNDAY MAY 3, 1863, GEN. NATHAN BEDFORD FORREST, BY HIS INDOMITABLE WILL, AFTER A RUNNING FIGHT OF 3 DAYS AND NIGHTS, WITH 410 MEN, CAPTURED COL. A. D. STREIGHT'S RAIDERS, NUMBERING 1600, THEREBY SAVING ROME FROM DESTRUCTION.[169]

APPENDIX D

The Forrest Equestrian Monument at Memphis, Tennessee

FROM *HISTORIC SOUTHERN MONUMENTS*, 1911

N. B. Forrest Equestrian Monument, Memphis, Tennessee, 1905

INSCRIPTIONS ON MONUMENT

South Front
NATHAN BEDFORD FORREST
1821-1877

West Front
1904
ERECTED BY HIS COUNTRYMEN IN HONOR
OF THE MILITARY GENIUS OF
LIEUTENANT-GENERAL NATHAN BEDFORD FORREST.
CONFEDERATE STATES ARMY
1861-1865

East Front
THOSE HOOF BEATS DIE NOT UPON FAME'S
CRIMSONED SOD,
BUT WILL RING THROUGH HER SONG AND HER STORY;
HE FOUGHT LIKE A TITAN AND STRUCK LIKE A GOD,
AND HIS DUST IS OUR ASHES OF GLORY.

MEMPHIS, TENN.
EQUESTRIAN STATUE OF FORREST

By Bettie Alder Calhoun Emerson
1911

The height of the entire monument is 22 feet. The height of the bronze figure is 9 feet, and it weighs ninety-five hundred pounds. The cost of the structure approximates thirty-three thousand dollars.

In Forrest Park, Memphis, Tenn., surrounded by fifteen thousand spectators, at 2.30 P. M. on May 16 little Miss Kathleen Bradley pulled the cord that released the veil from the magnificent equestrian statue of her illustrious great-grandfather, Lieutenant-General Nathan Bedford Forrest. There was a momentary silence as the imposing grandeur of this colossal bronze figure of the great "Wizard of the Saddle" and his steed met the gaze of the expectant crowd, then a wild cheer broke from hundreds of his old surviving followers clustered around the base and was enthusiastically taken up by the vast multitude.

The idea of erecting a monument to General Forrest was first projected in 1886, but it was not until 1891 that it took definite shape and a monument association was organized for this purpose. On November 18, 1900, the design was accepted and the order was given to the sculptor, Charles H. Niehaus. The designer of the base was Mr. B. C. Alsup, and it is built of Tennessee marble. The statue, which was made in Europe, arrived in Memphis on April 16, and was placed on its base a day or two later.

The unveiling of the monument was attended with elaborate ceremonies. In the big parade were most of the surviving staff officers of General Forrest, his general officers, and many of his old veterans who rode with him from 1861 to 1865. Judge J.

P. Young, who was one of Forrest's old troopers, was master of ceremonies. In opening the proceedings he said in part:

> No one who did not ride with Forrest can have so keen an appreciation of the personal qualities of the man as those who were actually under his direct command, and who, from daily, hourly observation, witnessed his fertility of resource, his vehemence in battle and his soulful tenderness toward the stricken soldier, whether friend or foe. But it was no holiday parade. It cost something to ride with Forrest. It meant days and nights of sleepless toil and motion. It meant countless miles under a burning sun in the choking dust. It meant limitless leagues across icy wastes, with a blanket of snow at night for a covering. It meant to run down and destroy miles of freighted supply trains, to burn depots of stores, to scale the parapets of redoubts, and to plunge, mounted, into the seeming vortex of hell, lighted with the fires of a myriad rifles and scores of belching guns.
>
> > "It meant to meet death face to face like a drillmaster, to look into his dread eyes, to toy with the horrid trappings of his trade, to scorn the deadly chill of his breath, and to turn away unscathed or sink into the oblivion of his eternal embrace."

Of the many eloquent tributes paid to the great soldier that day, one of the most significant was that spoken by [Yankee] Colonel C. A. Stanton, of the 3d Iowa Cavalry, 1861-1865, who for two years was directly opposed to General Forrest. He realized Forrest's methods of war at Brice's Cross Roads, Ripley, Harrisburg, Old Town Creek, Tallahatchie, and Hurricane Creek.

The spectacle of an officer who had fought in the Federal army delivering an address at the unveiling of a Confederate monument was an interesting one, and when Colonel Stanton was introduced the applause was most generous. Colonel Stanton said in part:

"During the war between the States I served four years in the Federal army, and what I learned then prompts what I now shall say. My knowledge of General Forrest's military career was acquired while for a part of two years with the Federal forces that were directly opposed to him and his command.

"General Forrest possessed the characteristic traits of the successful soldier; his personal bravery was without limit; his resources seemed to be endless, and his decisions, like Napoleon's, were instantaneous; he was aggressive, masterful, resolute, and self-reliant in the most perilous emergency; he was comprehensive in his grasp of every situation, supremely confident in himself and in his men, and inspired by his presence and example his soldiers fought as desperately as did Hannibal's fierce cavalry at Canne or the trained veterans of Caesar's Tenth Legion at Pharsalia. I think the battle at Brice's Cross Roads in June, 1864, was one of the best illustrations of General Forrest's daring courage, his ability in a critical moment to decide swiftly, his relentless vigor of action, and his intuitive perception of the time and place to strike fierce, stunning blows which fell like thunderbolts upon his enemy and won for him in this battle an overwhelming victory over an opposing force which greatly outnumbered his command.

"Impartial history has given General Forrest high rank as one of the greatest cavalry leaders of modern times. No

American, North or South, now seeks to lessen the measure of his fame, and no one can speak of him without, remembrance of the men who served with him and whose soldierly qualities made it possible for him to win his wonderful victories. No military leader was ever supported by more faithful, gallant, and daring subordinate officers. It has been truly said that 'the spirit of the cavalier which was found in the Southern armies was combined with the steadfastness of Cromwell's Ironsides,' and it is equally true that no soldiers, ever met more promptly every demand made upon them; no soldiers ever faced the enemies' blazing guns more fearlessly or performed greater feats of valor than did the veterans of Forrest's regiments in battles which were as hard-fought as Marathon or Philippi.

"The men who wore the gray from 1861 to 1865 still treasure the memories of those heroic days; but through all the years since that time they have contributed their full share to the advancement and prosperity of our common country, and to-day the nation has no truer friends than the ex-Confederate soldiers of the South.

"The war of 1861-1865 was a mighty conflict which stands without a parallel in the annals of time. Shiloh, Stone's River, Franklin, Chickamauga, and Gettysburg are names made sacred by the deeds done there and by the dead who lie there side by side in common graves, where the gray cloth and the blue have faded into dust alike.

> "This monument is history in bronze; it illustrates an eventful era in our national history; it commemorates General Forrest's fame and it represents all the gallant soldiers of his command; it attests the splendid courage which won triumphant victories and did not fail when reverses came; it stands for heroic deeds which are now the proud heritage of all American citizens. It is eminently fitting that this figure should stand here within the borders of the Volunteer State, whose soldiers have marched and fought 'from valley's depth to mountain height and from inland rivers to the sea,' in every war in the history of our republic, with a valor which has helped to make the name and fame of the American soldier immortal."

Mr. Niehaus, the sculptor, is an artist of national reputation, and has a long list of statues and monuments to his credit. The Forrest monument is one of his best.

There is always a peculiar interest that attaches to the making of a statue, and to no one part of it more than to the models. The General Forrest statue, being equestrian, had two models—a man and a horse. The man, though a professional model, is as much *sui generis* as the character he simulated; a Prussian cavalry officer, a fire-eater and a superb horseman, he fitted the part so well that it became a matter of diplomacy to keep the peace while he was posing, for he seemed to have a good American chip on his shoulder all the time.

The horse that posed for the statue was the fourth one selected, all the others being abandoned after a trial of months. The handsome animal who held the job, however, is a full brother of Lord Derby, and of the distinguished Mambrino Chief pedigree. He is jet black, full of spirit, and yet docile, and was easily taught to hold required positions by tips of carrots, apples and sugar.

He also posed for the statue of St. Louis at the Louisiana Purchase Exposition, and is now (1905) doing duty for a statue that is to go on Riverside Drive when completed. His name is "Commander," and he was purchased especially for the General Forrest model.

Fortunately for the artist, the tailor who made General Forrest's clothes had kept his measurements, and it not only enabled a uniform to be made accurately, but furnished accurate measurements that cannot always be obtained from photographs and uncertain testimony. An actual replica of his sword was made and the horse's trappings were copied from originals.[170]

APPENDIX E

A Brief Biography of Nathan Bedford Forrest

BY BETTIE ALDER CALHOUN EMERSON
1911

Born in Bedford County, Tenn., July 13, 1821; died at Memphis, Tenn., October 29, 1877. He removed to Hernando, Miss., in 1842, and was a planter until 1852, when he removed to Memphis.

General Forrest was one of the most remarkable men developed by the war. In fighting he was the Stonewall Jackson of the West. United States Senator John W. Daniel, of Virginia, in his great speech as orator for the United Confederate Veterans, at their reunion in New Orleans in April, 1892, said:

> Forrest, the "Wizard of the Saddle"! Oh, what genius was in that wonderful man. He felt the field as Blind Tom touches the keys of the piano.[171] "War means killing," he said, "and the way to kill is to get there first with the most men." There is military science—Napoleon, Stonewall, Lee—in a nutshell. He was not taught at West Point, but he gave lessons to West Point.[172]

NOTES

1. See Jones, TDMV, pp. 144, 200-201, 273.
2. See Seabrook, TAHSR, passim. See also, Pollard, LC, p. 178; J. H. Franklin, pp. 101, 111, 130, 149; Nicolay and Hay, ALCW, Vol. 1, p. 627.
3. For a detailed discussion on this topic, see Seabrook, LW, passim.
4. See e.g., Seabrook, TQJD, pp. 30, 38, 76.
5. Seabrook, EYWTATCWIW, p. 13.
6. Dunn and Dobzhansky, p. 105. For a late 19th-Century view on this topic, see W. T. Alexander, pp. 21-24.
7. Montague, TCOR, p. 11.
8. Acts 17:24, 26. Jesus also disregarded race, as he illustrated when he met the woman of Samaria at Jacob's Well in Sychar. The Samaritans were of "mixed race" and Jews were forbidden to associate with them. See John 4:5-10.
9. See Dunn and Dobzhansky, pp. 6-7.
10. W. T. Alexander, pp. 21-23.
11. See Dunn and Dobzhansky, pp. 16-17. It is interesting to note here that motor ability and emotional balance tests reveal that 50 percent of the differences between twins are due to environmental factors; less than half are due to heredity. Dunn and Dobzhansky, p. 22.
12. Montague, MMDM, p. 44.
13. Montague, TCOR, p. xiii.
14. Montague, SOR, pp. 150-151.
15. Dunn and Dobzhansky, p. 14.
16. Montague, TCOR, pp. 17, 23.
17. See Mead, SATCOR, passim. See also Dahlberg, passim. For an early 20th-Century discussion on the falsity of "race," see Beard, pp. 229-263.
18. Alland, p. 128.
19. For more on why Forrest will always be idolized in the South, see Seabrook, ARB, passim.
20. According to the U.S. Census Bureau, European-Americans are now a minority in the states of Texas, Hawaii, California, and New Mexico.
21. For more on this topic, see my book of the same name.
22. Connell, p. 217. (This statement appears to be a paraphrasal of the author.)
23. Hodge, Vol. 2, s.v. "Race Names" (p. 353). The phrase literally means "negro's kinsman."
24. Due to the fact that Liberal authors and publishers do not recognize any form of racism except white racism, red racism is difficult to find in American literature. However it is not impossible. As one example of Indian racism toward whites, see Lundquist, p. 161.
25. Seabrook, EYWTAASIW, pp. 680-681.
26. See e.g., Moraga and Anzaldúa, p. 44, and Seabrook, EYWTAASIW, pp. 681-684.
27. Lafayette De Mente, p. 145.
28. I researched a book recently in which the Liberal (read "anti-white") author proclaimed that "it is impossible for whites to experience racial discrimination."
29. Seabrook, EYWTAASIW, p. 742.
30. Seabrook, AL, passim.
31. Seabrook, TQNBF, pp. 100-101. Emphasis added.
32. Seabrook, ARB, p. 437.
33. Seabrook, TQNBF, p. 107. Emphasis added.
34. It is my opinion that those who are preoccupied with race, racism, and skin color are latent racists, and that they pretend to fight against racism in order to conceal it, both from themselves and from others.
35. Seabrook, TQNBF, p. 109.
36. Seabrook, TQNBF, pp. 114-116. Emphasis added.
37. Seabrook, ARB, pp. 547-548. My paraphrasal.
38. Seabrook, ARB, p. 213.
39. See e.g., B. F. Butler, p. 903. Many other famous Northerners also did not believe in abolition or equality of the races, such as General William T. Sherman. See e.g., Seabrook, EYWTACWW, p. 175.
40. Seabrook, ARB, p. 548.
41. Seabrook, ARB, p. 26.
42. Seabrook, ARB, pp. 466-467.
43. Seabrook, ARB, p. 12.

44. Seabrook, CFF, p. 166.
45. Seabrook, CFF, p. 182.
46. Seabrook, EYWTAASIW, pp. 55-57.
47. Only one notable exception comes to mind: no evidence of slavery has ever been found in the ruins of the Minoans of ancient Crete.
48. Seabrook, EYWTAASIW, passim.
49. See e.g., Galatians 3:28.
50. Mish, s.v. "race." See also Ox. E.D., s.v. "Race."
51. The word racism was first coined, not by Leon Trotsky (in 1927) or Ruth Benedict (in 1939), as is commonly believed, but by U.S. Colonel Richard Henry Pratt in 1902. That year Pratt used the word during a speech before a conference in New York concerning Native-Americans: "Segregating any class or race of people apart from the rest of the people kills the progress of the segregated people or makes their growth very slow. Association of races and classes is necessary to destroy racism and classism." See Barrows, 20th Annual Meeting, 4th Session, 1902, p. 134. See also Ox. E.D., s.v. "Race."
52. Seabrook, EYWTAASIW, pp. 120-165.
53. Genesis 37:18-36.
54. Seabrook, EYWTAASIW, pp. 400-418.
55. See Article 1, Section 2, Clause 3; Article 1, Section 9, Clause 1; Article 4, Section 2, Clause 3.
56. Seabrook, EYWTAASIW, pp. 244-248.
57. See e.g., Halliburton, passim.
58. Seabrook, EYWTAASIW, pp. 248-250.
59. Seabrook, EYWTAASIW, pp. 155-163.
60. Seabrook, EYWTAASIW, pp. 62-119, 867. As I write these words the headlines are filled with news about the ongoing enslavement and torture of thousands of people (of all races, ages, and nationalities—including fellow native Africans) across Africa.
61. Seabrook, EYWTAASIW, pp. 182-183.
62. Seabrook, EYWTAASIW, p. 183.
63. Seabrook, EYWTAASIW, pp. 169, 654, 871.
64. Seabrook, EYWTAASIW, pp. 215-216.
65. See Seabrook, EYWTAASIW, passim; Seabrook, S101, passim.
66. For more on this topic, see Seabrook, TGYC, passim.
67. See Seabrook, EYWTAASIW, pp. 860-863.
68. Seabrook, ARB, p. 220.
69. Seabrook, ARB, p. 220.
70. Nicolay and Hay, ALCW, Vol. 1, p. 288. Emphasis added.
71. Seabrook, ARB, p. 71.
72. Seabrook, ARB, p. 214.
73. Seabrook, ARB, p. 71.
74. Seabrook, ARB, pp. 214-215.
75. Seabrook, ARB, p. 215.
76. Seabrook, ARB, p. 221. Emphasis added.
77. Seabrook, NBFATKKK, p. 19.
78. Seabrook, EYWTATCWIW, p. 158.
79. Seabrook, EYWTAASIW, p. 785.
80. Seabrook, EYWTATCWIW, pp. 158-159.
81. Sadly, their exact number will never be known because Yankees, like war criminal General Edward Hatch, specifically targeted Southern courthouses—where records were kept—for burning.
82. Seabrook, ARB, p. 259.
83. Seabrook, TQNBF, p. 101. Emphasis added. It is little wonder that Forrest and other Southern slave owners did not want their servants to run away. This was not because of despotism and sadism, as pro-North historians claim, but rather because of financial investment. The General's 45 black Confederate soldiers, for example, were worth a total of at least $2,250,000 in today's currency. When he finally emancipated them all in 1863, he willingly forfeited this massive investment in exchange for the liberty of his loyal servants. Forrest's immense financial sacrifice was well understood by them and was returned in kind when nearly all of them returned to work for him after the War.
84. Seabrook, ARB, p. 259. Emphasis added.
85. Seabrook, ARB, pp. 26, 144.
86. See e.g., Jordan and Pryor, p. 296.
87. See e.g., Jordan and Pryor, pp. 524-525.
88. Seabrook, TQNBF, pp. 31-32.
89. For more on these topics, see Seabrook, AL, passim.

90. Seabrook, TQNBF, pp. 32-33. Emphasis added.
91. See Seabrook, EYWTAASIW, pp. 722-723.
92. See ORA, Ser. 1, Vol. 39, Pt. 1, p. 545.
93. Seabrook, TQNBF, pp. 81-82.
94. See Article 4, Section 2, Clause 3 of the original U.S. Constitution. The passage of the Thirteenth Amendment in December 1865, which finally outlawed American slavery, made the Fugitive Slave Law obsolete.
95. In the 1850s one could receive a six month prison sentence and a fine of up to $1,000 for ignoring or breaking the Fugitive Slave Law (though more typically it was a 20 day jail sentence and a $100 fine). See e.g., Cochran, pp. 95, 151-156. As a military officer during the War Forrest may or may not have been subject to this regulation. Either way, as a firm supporter of the C.S. Constitution, by returning runaway slaves to their owners he was acting according to Confederate law (see Article 4, Section 2, Clause 3). See Seabrook, TCOTCSOA, p. 116.
96. Seabrook, ARB, p. 433.
97. Mathes, pp. 359-360. Edwards was known for his cruelty to animals as well. Only weeks prior to his death at Forrest's hands, the freedman had mercilessly beat a mule to death. On another occasion Edwards whipped his wife so badly that a doctor had to be called. Wills, pp. 325-326.
98. Seabrook, ARB, p. 434.
99. Seabrook, ARB, p. 434.
100. Seabrook, TQNBF, pp. 99-100. Emphasis added.
101. Seabrook, TQNBF, p. 108. Emphasis added.
102. Dickert, pp. 427-428. Emphasis added.
103. Seabrook, ARB, p. 504.
104. Seabrook, ARB, p. 259.
105. Seabrook, ARB, pp. 26, 144.
106. Seabrook, ARB, pp. 51, 101, 155, 306-307, 341, 368, 461.
107. Seabrook, NBFATBOFP, pp. 18-19.
108. Seabrook, NBFATBOFP, p. 19.
109. Jordan and Pryor, p. 431.
110. Seabrook, NBFATBOFP, pp. 20-21.
111. According to Forrest's cavalry chaplain, Dr. David C. Kelley, the General "had repeatedly told him that it was not his policy to kill captured negroes, but, on the contrary, to handle them well and return them to their owners . . ." Morton, p. 191.
112. Seabrook, NBFATBOFP, p. 21.
113. ORA, Ser. 1, Vol. 39, Pt. 1, p. 229. Among the "dastardly Yankee reporters" Forrest alludes to were those who worked for pro-Union Southern newspapers, such as the scallywag-run Memphis *Bulletin*, which helped nurture the "Fort Pillow Massacre" myth in a series of pro-North articles that began on April 13, 1864. Seabrook, NBFATBOFP, p. 21.
114. Seabrook, NBFATBOFP, pp. 21-22. Emphasis added. Two months after Fort Pillow Forrest himself wrote: "Since the war began, I have captured many thousand Federal prisoners, and they, including the survivors of the 'Fort Pillow Massacre,' black and white, are living witnesses of the fact, that, with my knowledge or consent, or by my orders, not one of them has ever been insulted or maltreated in any way." Jordan and Pryor, p. 491.
115. Seabrook, NBFATBOFP, p. 23.
116. Seabrook, ARB, p. 335.
117. Seabrook, NBFATBOFP, p. 25.
118. Seabrook, NBFATBOFP, p. 25.
119. Seabrook, NBFATBOFP, p. 43.
120. Seabrook, NBFATBOFP, p. 43.
121. Seabrook, NBFATBOFP, p. 45.
122. Seabrook, NBFATBOFP, pp. 45-46.
123. Seabrook, NBFATBOFP, pp. 47-48.
124. Seabrook, NBFATBOFP, p. 55.
125. Seabrook, ARB, pp. 364-365.
126. Seabrook, NBFATBOFP, pp. 55-56.
127. For more on this topic, see Seabrook, AL, passim.
128. Seabrook, ARB, pp. 364-365. Emphasis added.
129. Seabrook, NBFATBOFP, pp. 56-57.
130. Jordan and Pryor, p. 440.
131. Seabrook, NBFATBOFP, p. 79.
132. Seabrook, NBFATBOFP, p. 31.
133. Seabrook, NBFATKKK, p. 41.
134. Seabrook, NBFATKKK, p. 113.
135. Seabrook, NBFATKKK, pp. 45-100.

136. Seabrook, NBFATKKK, pp. 44, 108.
137. Seabrook, NBFATKKK, pp. 29-30. Emphasis added.
138. Seabrook, NBFATKKK, p. 30. Emphasis added.
139. Seabrook, NBFATKKK, p. 30. Emphasis added.
140. Seabrook, NBFATKKK, p. 109.
141. Seabrook, NBFATKKK, pp. 15, 102.
142. Jordan and Pryor, pp. ix, xi.
143. Seabrook, NBFATKKK, p. 15.
144. Seabrook, NBFATKKK, p. 111.
145. Seabrook, NBFATKKK, p. 112.
146. Seabrook, NBFATKKK, p. 30.
147. Seabrook, NBFATKKK, passim.
148. Seabrook, ARB, pp. 451, 578.
149. Seabrook, NBFATKKK, p. 112.
150. Seabrook, NBFATKKK, pp. 112-113.
151. Seabrook, NBFATKKK, p. 113.
152. Seabrook, NBFATKKK, p. 114.
153. Seabrook, NBFATKKK, pp. 114-115.
154. Seabrook, NBFATKKK, p. 115. Emphasis added.
155. Rose, pp. 22-23. Emphasis added.
156. Seabrook, TQNBF, p. 105. Emphasis added.
157. Seabrook, TQNBF, p. 106. Emphasis added.
158. Seabrook, TQNBF, p. 111.
159. Seabrook, TQNBF, pp. 111-112.
160. For the truth about the South's original Reconstruction KKK, see Seabrook, NBFATKKK, passim.
161. Seabrook, TQNBF, p. 100.
162. Seabrook, TQNBF, p. 109.
163. Seabrook, TQNBF, p. 109.
164. Mathes, p. 373. Emphasis added.
165. *Confederate Veteran*, Vol. 13, No. 9, September 1903, p. 421.
166. Seabrook, TQNBF, pp. 114-116. Emphasis added.
167. *Confederate Veteran*, Vol. 3, No. 8, August 1895, p. 226.
168. Seabrook, NBFATBOFP, p. 97.
169. Emerson, pp. 116-118.
170. Emerson, pp. 313-320.
171. Thomas "Blind Tom" Wiggins was a poplar blind African-American entertainer from Georgia, who dazzled Victorian crowds with his virtuoso piano performances.
172. Emerson, pp. 319-320.

BIBLIOGRAPHY

Alexander, William T. *History of the Colored Race in America*. Kansas City, MO: Palmetto Publishing Co., 1899.

Alland, Alexander, Jr. *Human Diversity*. Garden City, NY: Anchor Books, 1973.

Baepler, Paul (ed.). *White Slaves, African Masters: An Anthology of American Barbary Captivity Narratives*. Chicago, IL: University of Chicago Press, 1999.

Ballagh, James Curtis. *White Servitude in the Colony of Virginia: A Study of the System of Indentured Servitude in the American Colonies*. Whitefish, MT: Kessinger Publishing, 2004.

Barrow, Charles Kelly, J. H. Segars, and R. B. Rosenburg (eds.). *Black Confederates*. 1995. Gretna, LA: Pelican Publishing Co., 2001 ed.

———. *Forgotten Confederates: An Anthology About Black Southerners*. Saint Petersburg, FL: Southern Heritage Press, 1997.

Barrows, Isabel C. (ed.). *Proceedings of the Twentieth Annual Meeting of the Lake Mohonk Conference of Friends of the Indian*. Lake Mohonk, NY: The Lake Mohonk Conference, 1902.

Beard, Charles A. (ed.). *Whither Mankind: A Panorama of Modern Civilization*. New York, NY: Longmans, Green and Co., 1928.

Bekkaoui, Khalid. *White Women Captives in North Africa: Narratives of Enslavement, 1735-1830*. New York, NY: Macmillan, 2011.

Bennett, Lerone, Jr. *Forced Into Glory: Abraham Lincoln's White Dream*. Chicago, IL: Johnson Publishing Co., 2000.

Boyde, Henry. *Several Voyages to Barbary: Containing an Historical and Geographical Account of the Country, With the Hardships, Sufferings, and Manner of Redeeming Christian Slaves*. London, UK: Olive Payne, 1736.

Browder, Earl. *Lincoln and the Communists*. New York, NY: Workers Library Publishers, Inc., 1936.

Butler, Benjamin Franklin. *Butler's Book (Autobiography and Personal Reminiscences of Major-General Benjamin F. Butler: A Review of His Legal, Political, and Military Career)*. Boston, MA: A. M. Thayer and Co., 1892.

Cobden, John C. *The White Slaves of England*. New York, NY: C. M. Saxton, Barker and Co., 1860.

Cochran, William C. (ed.). *The Western Reserve Historical Society*. Publication No. 101, January 1920. Cleveland, OH: TWRHS, 1920.

Connell, Evan S. *Son of the Morning Star: Custer and the Little Big Horn*. 1984. New York, NY: North Point Press, 1997 ed.

Cooley, Henry S. *A Study of Slavery in New Jersey*. Baltimore, MD: Johns Hopkins University Press, 1896.

Cooper, Frederick. *Plantation Slavery on the East Coast of Africa.* New Haven, CT: Yale University Press, 1977.

Cox, Earnest Sevier. *White America: The American Racial Problem As Seen in a Worldwide Perspective and Lincoln's Negro Policy.* Richmond, VA: White America Society, 1923.

Dahlberg, Gunnar. *Race, Reason and Rubbish: A Primer of Race Biology.* New York, NY: Columbia University Press, 1942.

Davis, Robert C. *Christian Slaves, Muslim Masters: White Slavery in the Mediterranean, the Barbary Coast and Italy, 1500-1800.* New York, NY: Macmillan, 2004.

Davis, Simon. *Race Relations in Ancient Egypt: Greek, Egyptian, Hebrew, Roman.* London, UK: Methuen, 1953.

Dickert, D. Augustus. *History of Kershaw's Brigade, With Complete Roll of Companies, Biographical Sketches, Incidents, Anecdotes, Etc.* Newberry, SC: Elbert H. Aull Co., 1899.

Dunn, Leslie C., and Theodosius Dobzhansky. *Heredity, Race and Society: A Scientific Explanation of Human Differences.* 1946. New York, NY: Mentor, 1949 ed.

Emerson, Bettie Alder Calhoun. *Historic Southern Monuments: Representative Memorials of the Heroic Dead of the Southern Confederacy.* New York, NY: Neale Publishing Co., 1911.

Evans, Clement Anselm (ed.). *Confederate Military History.* 12 vols. Atlanta, GA: Confederate Publishing Co., 1899.

Farrow, Anne, Joel Lang, and Jennifer Frank. *Complicity: How the North Promoted, Prolonged, and Profited From Slavery.* New York, NY: Ballantine, 2005.

Fisher, N. R. E. *Slavery in Classical Greece.* London, UK: Bristol Classical Press, 1993.

Foote, Thelma Wills. *Black and White Manhattan: The History of Racial Formation in Colonial New York City.* New York, NY: Oxford University Press, 2004.

Franklin, John Hope. *Reconstruction After the Civil War.* Chicago, IL: University of Chicago Press, 1961.

Galenson, David W. *White Servitude in Colonial America.* New York, NY: Cambridge University Press, 1981.

Gallay, Alan (ed.). *Indian Slavery in Colonial America.* Lincoln, NE: University of Nebraska, 2009.

Halliburton, R. *Red Over Black: Black Slavery Among the Cherokee Indians.* Westport, CT: Greenwood Press, 1977.

Hildreth, Richard. *The White Slave: Another Picture of Slave Life in America.* London, UK: George Rutledge and Co., 1852.

Hodge, Frederick Webb (ed.). *Handbook of American Indians North of Mexico.* 2 vols. Washington, D.C.: Government Printing Office, 1910.

Hoffman, Michael A., II. *They Were White and They Were Slaves: The Untold History of the Enslavement of Whites in Early America.* Dresden, NY: Wiswell Ruffin House, 1993.

Johnston, William D. *Slavery in Rhode Island, 1755-1776.* Providence, RI: Rhode Island Historical Society, 1894.

Johnstone, Huger William. *Truth of War Conspiracy, 1861.* Idylwild, GA: H. W. Johnstone, 1921.

Jones, John William. *The Davis Memorial Volume; Or Our Dead President, Jefferson Davis and*

      the World's Tribute to His Memory. Richmond, VA: B. F. Johnson, 1889.
Jordan, Don, and Michael Walsh. *White Cargo: The Forgotten History of Britain's White Slaves in America*. New York, NY: New York University Press, 2008.
Jordan, Ervin L. *Black Confederates and Afro-Yankees in Civil War Virginia*. Charlottesville, VA: University Press of Virginia, 1995.
Jordan, Thomas, and John P. Pryor. *The Campaigns of General Nathan Bedford Forrest and of Forrest's Cavalry*. New Orleans, LA: Blelock and Co., 1868.
Lafayette De Mente, Boyé. *The Chinese Have a Word for It: The Complete Guide to Chinese Thought and Culture*. New York, NY: McGraw-Hill, 2000.
Latham, Henry. *Black and White: A Journal of a Three Months' Tour in the United States*. Philadelphia, PA: Lippincott, 1867.
Lemire, Elise. *Black Walden: Slavery and Its Aftermath in Concord, Massachusetts*. Philadelphia, PA: University of Pennsylvania Press, 2009.
Lundquist, Suzanne Evertsen. *Native American Literatures: An Introduction*. New York, NY: Continuum, 2004.
Manegold, C. S. *Ten Hills Farm: The Forgotten History of Slavery in the North*. Princeton, NJ: Princeton University Press, 2010.
Mann, Horace. *Slavery and the Slave-Trade in the District of Columbia*. Speech delivered in the House of Representatives of the United States, February 23, 1849. Philadelphia, PA: Merrihew and Thompson (printers), 1849.
Marsh, Edward G. (ed.). *Account of the Slavery of Friends in the Barbary States, Towards the Close of the Seventeenth Century*. London, UK: Edward G. Marsh, 1848.
Mathes, James Harvey. *General Forrest*. New York, NY: D. Appleton and Co., 1902.
McCarty, Burke (ed.). *Little Sermons In Socialism by Abraham Lincoln*. Chicago, IL: The Chicago Daily Socialist, 1910.
McManus, Edgar J. *A History of Negro Slavery in New York*. Syracuse, NY: Syracuse University Press, 1966.
——. *Black Bondage in the North*. Syracuse, NY: Syracuse University Press, 1973.
Mead, Margaret. *Science and the Concept of Race*. New York, NY: Columbia University Press, 1968.
Meltzer, Milton. *Slavery: A World History*. 2 vols. in 1. 1971. New York, NY: Da Capo Press, 1993 ed.
Mendelsohn, I. *Slavery in the Ancient Near East: A Comparative Study of Slavery in Babylonia, Assyria, Syria, Palestine, from the Middle of the Third Millennium*. New York, NY: Oxford University Press, 1949.
Meriwether, Elizabeth Avery. *Facts and Falsehoods Concerning the War on the South, 1861-1865*. (Originally written under the pseudonym "George Edmonds.") Memphis, TN: A. R. Taylor, 1904.
Min, Pyong Gap (ed.). *Encyclopedia of Racism in the United States*. 3 vols. Westport, CT: Greenwood Press, 2005.
Minges, Patrick N. *Slavery in the Cherokee Nation: The Keetoowah Society and the Defining of a People, 1855-1867*. New York, NY: Routledge, 2003.
Minor, Charles Landon Carter. *The Real Lincoln: From the Testimony of His Contemporaries*. Richmond, VA: Everett Waddey Co., 1904.
Milton, Giles. *White Gold: The Extraordinary Story of Thomas Pellow and Islam's One Million White Slaves*. New York, NY: Farrar, Straus, and Giroux, 2005.

Mish, Frederick (ed.). *Webster's Ninth New Collegiate Dictionary*. Springfield, MA: Merriam-Webster, 1984.

Montague, Ashley. *Man's Most Dangerous Myth: The Fallacy of Race*. 1942. Walnut Creek, CA: AltaMira Press, 1997 ed.

——. *Statement on Race*. 1951. New York, NY: Oxford University Press, 1972 ed.

——. (ed.) *The Concept of Race*. 1964. London, UK: Collier Books, 1969 ed.

Moore, George Henry. *Notes on the History of Slavery in Massachusetts*. New York, NY: D. Appleton and Co., 1866.

Moraga, Cherrie, and Gloria Anzaldúa (eds.). *This Bridge Called My Back: Writings by Radical Women of Color*. Albany, NY: State University of New York Press, 2015.

Morton, John Watson. *The Artillery of Nathan Bedford Forrest: The Wizard of the Saddle*. Nashville, TN, M. E. Church, 1909.

Nicolay, John George, and John Hay (eds.). *Abraham Lincoln: Complete Works*. 12 vols. New York, NY: The Century Co., 1907.

Norris, Robert. *A Short Account of the African Slave Trade*. London, UK: W. Lowndes, 1789.

Northrup, Ansel Judd. *Slavery in New York*. (Article from the *State Library Bulletin*, "History," No. 4, May 1900.) New York, NY: University of the State of New York, 1900.

Oates, William Calvin. *The War Between the Union and the Confederacy and Its Lost Opportunities*. New York, NY: Neale Publishing Co., 1905.

ORA (full title: *The War of the Rebellion: A Compilation of the Official Records of the Union and Confederate Armies*. (Multiple volumes.) Washington, D.C.: Government Printing Office, 1880.

ORN (full title: *Official Records of the Union and Confederate Navies in the War of the Rebellion*). (Multiple volumes.) Washington, D.C.: Government Printing Office, 1894.

Perbi, Akosua Adoma. *A History of Indigenous Slavery in Ghana: From the 15th to the 19th Century*. Legon-Accra Ghana, West Africa: Sub-Saharan Publishers, 2004.

Pollard, Edward Alfred. *The Lost Cause*. New York, NY: E. B. Treat and Co., 1867.

Reed, Wallace P. (ed.). *History of Atlanta, Georgia, with Illustrations and Biographical Sketches of Some of Its Prominent Men and Pioneers*. Syracuse, NY: D. Mason and Co., 1889.

Robertson, Claire, and Martin A. Klein (eds.). *Women and Slavery in Africa*. Madison, WI: University of Wisconsin Press, 1983.

Rose, S. E. F. *The Ku Klux Klan or Invisible Empire*. New Orleans, LA: L. Graham Co., 1914.

Ruby, Robert. H. *Indian Slavery in the Pacific Northwest*. Glendale, CA: Arthur H. Clark, 1993.

Seabrook, Lochlainn. *Abraham Lincoln: The Southern View*. 2007. Franklin, TN: Sea Raven Press, 2013 ed.

——. *A Rebel Born: A Defense of Nathan Bedford Forrest*. 2010. Franklin, TN: Sea Raven Press, 2011 ed.

——. *Everything You Were Taught About the Civil War is Wrong, Ask a Southerner!* 2010. Franklin, TN: Sea Raven Press, revised 2014 ed.

——. *The Quotable Jefferson Davis: Selections From the Writings and Speeches of the Confederacy's First President*. Franklin, TN: Sea Raven Press, 2011.

———. *Lincolnology: The Real Abraham Lincoln Revealed In His Own Words.* Franklin, TN: Sea Raven Press, 2011.

———. *The Unquotable Abraham Lincoln: The President's Quotes They Don't Want You To Know!* Franklin, TN: Sea Raven Press, 2011.

———. *The Quotable Nathan Bedford Forrest: Selections From the Writings and Speeches of the Confederacy's Most Brilliant Cavalryman.* Franklin, TN: Sea Raven Press, 2012 Sesquicentennial Civil War Edition.

———. *The Great Impersonator: 99 Reasons to Dislike Abraham Lincoln.* Franklin, TN: Sea Raven Press, 2012.

———. *The Constitution of the Confederate States of America Explained: A Clause-by-Clause Study of the South's Magna Carta.* Franklin, TN: Sea Raven Press, 2012.

———. *The Alexander H. Stephens Reader: Excerpts From the Works of a Confederate Founding Father.* Franklin, TN: Sea Raven Press, 2013.

———. *Everything You Were Taught About American Slavery War is Wrong, Ask a Southerner!* Franklin, TN: Sea Raven Press, 2015.

———. *Slavery 101: Amazing Facts You Never Knew About American's "Peculiar Institution."* Franklin, TN: Sea Raven Press, 2015.

———. *Confederacy 101: Amazing Facts You Never Knew About America's Oldest Political Tradition.* Franklin, TN: Sea Raven Press, 2015.

———. *The Great Yankee Coverup: What the North Doesn't Want You to Know About Lincoln's War!* Franklin, TN: Sea Raven Press, 2015.

———. *Confederate Flag Facts: What Every American Should Know About Dixie's Southern Cross.* Franklin, TN: Sea Raven Press, 2015.

———. *Nathan Bedford Forrest and the Battle of Fort Pillow: Yankee Myth, Confederate Fact.* Franklin, TN: Sea Raven Press, 2015.

———. *Nathan Bedford Forrest and the Ku Klux Klan: Yankee Myth, Confederate Fact.* Franklin, TN: Sea Raven Press, 2015.

———. *Lincoln's War: The Real Cause, the Real Winner, the Real Loser.* Spring Hill, TN: Sea Raven Press, 2016.

Smith, Abbot Emerson. *Colonists in Bondage: White Servitude and Convict Labor in America, 1607-1776.* Chapel Hill, NC: University of North Carolina Press, 1947.

Sobel, Mechal. *The World They Made Together: Black and White Values in Eighteenth-Century Virginia.* Princeton, NJ: Princeton University Press, 1987.

Steiner, Bernard Christian. *History of Slavery in Connecticut.* Baltimore, MD: Johns Hopkins University Press, 1893.

Sumner, Charles. *White Slavery in the Barbary States: A Lecture Before the Boston Mercantile Library Association, Feb. 17, 1847.* Boston, MA: William D. Ticknor and Co., 1847.

The Oxford English Dictionary. 1971. Oxford, UK: Oxford University Press, 1980 compact ed.

Toy, John. *Slavery Indispensable to the Civilization of Africa.* Baltimore, MD: John Toy, 1855.

Turner, Edward Raymond. *Slavery in Pennsylvania: A Dissertation.* Baltimore, MD: The Lord Baltimore Press, 1911.

Ware, Camilla. *Slavery In Vermont, and in Other Parts of the United States.* Woodstock, VT: Davis and Greene, 1858.

INDEX

Adair, George W., 39, 40
Adams, Shelby L., 124
Akerstrom, J. C., 61
Alsup, B. C., 101
Anderson, Charles W., 60
Anderson, Loni, 124
Arthur, King, 123
Atkins, Chet, 124
Barnett, T. J., 69
Beauregard, Pierre G. T., 96, 124
Bernstein, Leonard, 124
Blind Tom, 107
Bolling, Edith, 124
Boone, Daniel, 124
Boone, Pat, 124
Booth, Lionel F., 56
Bradley, Kathleen Forrest, 101
Breckinridge, John C., 124
Brooke, Edward W., 124
Brooks, Preston S., 124
Brownlow, William G., 50, 69, 70
Buchanan, Patrick J., 124
Buford, Abe, 46
Buford, Abraham, 124
Butler, Andrew P., 124
Butler, Benjamin F., 29
Caesar, Julius, 103
Cain (Bible), 33
Campbell, Joseph, 123
Carson, Martha, 124
Carter, Theodrick "Tod", 124
Cash, Johnny, 124
Caudill, Benjamin E., 123
Chalmers, James R., 90
Chandler, Andrew Martin, 49
Chandler, Silas, 49
Cheairs, Nathaniel F., 124
Chesnut, Mary, 124
Clark, William, 124

Collis, Captain, 49
Columbus, Christopher, 23
Combs, Bertram T., 124
Crawford, Cindy, 124
Crockett, Davy, 124
Cromwell, Oliver, 104
Crowe, James R., 69, 70
Cruise, Tom, 124
Cyrus, Billy R., 124
Cyrus, Miley, 124
Daniel, John W., 107
Davis, Jefferson, 9, 11, 18, 30, 31, 43, 123, 124
Dickert, D. A., 52
Duncomb, Andrew J., 92
Duvall, Robert, 124
Edward I, King, 123
Edwards, Thomas "Tom", 48
Emerson, Bettie A. C., 101, 107
Falls, Ellis, 65
Fitch, Charles, 65
Foote, Shelby, 123
Forbes, Christopher, 124
Forrest, Nathan Bedford, 11, 18-22, 25-30, 32, 33, 35-41, 44-65, 67-87, 89-91, 93, 95-97, 99-107, 123, 124
Gayheart, Rebecca, 124
George III, King, 10
Gist, States R., 124
Gordon, George W., 71, 124
Grant, Ulysses S., 12, 35, 36, 61, 63, 64, 76, 83
Graves, Robert, 123
Griffith, Andy, 124
Guaraldi, Vince, 124
Hancock, Richard R., 54, 55
Harding, William G., 124
Hearn, Lafcadio, 39

Hitler, Adolf, 19, 83
Hood, John Bell, 124
Howard, Oliver O., 49
Hunter, L. C., 63
Hurlbut, Stephen A., 63
Jack the Ripper, 19
Jackson, Andrew, 124
Jackson, Henry R., 124
Jackson, Stonewall, 107, 124
Jacob (Bible), 33
James, Frank, 124
James, Jesse, 124
Jefferson, Thomas, 124
Jent, Elias, Sr., 123
Jerry, Forrest's body servant, 39
Jesus, 123
John, Elton, 124
Johnston, Joseph E., 11
Jones, J. Calvin, 71
Jones, Winfield, 75
Jordan, Thomas, 39, 58
Joseph (Bible), 33
Judd, Ashley, 124
Judd, Naomi, 124
Judd, Wynonna, 124
Kautz, August V., 42
Kennedy, John B., 70, 74, 76
Lee, Fitzhugh, 124
Lee, Robert E., 107, 124
Lee, Stephen D., 124
Lee, William H. F., 124
Lester, John C., 70
Lewis, Lou, 27
Lewis, Meriwether, 124
Lincoln, 56
Lincoln, Abraham, 9, 12, 15, 18, 24, 26, 29-31, 37, 43, 45, 46, 49, 53, 55, 58, 61-64, 69, 76
Longstreet, James, 11, 124
Loveless, Patty, 124
Manigault, Arthur M., 124

Manigault, Joseph, 124
Marvin, Lee, 124
Maury, Abram P., 124
McCord, Frank O., 70
McGavock, Caroline E. (Winder), 124
McGavock, David H., 124
McGavock, Emily, 124
McGavock, Francis, 124
McGavock, James R., 124
McGavock, John W., 124
McGavock, Lysander, 124
McGavock, Randal W., 124
McGraw, Tim, 124
Meriwether, Elizabeth A., 124
Meriwether, Minor, 124
Montagu, Ashley, 13
Morgan, John H., 124
Morton, John W., 124
Mosby, John S., 124
Mussolini, Benito, 19
Napoleon, 107
Nelson, Louis N., 48
Newson, Gregory, 122
Niehaus, Charles H., 101, 105
Nugent, Ted, 124
Paine, Ora Susan, 71
Parton, Dolly, 124
Paul, Saint, 12
Perkins, Jerry, 50
Pettus, Edmund W., 124
Pillow, Gideon J., 124
Polk, James K., 124
Polk, Leonidas, 124
Polk, Lucius E., 124
Presley, Elvis, 124
Pryor, J. P., 39, 58
Rachel (Bible), 33
Randolph, Edmund J., 124
Randolph, George W., 124
Ray, John F., 61
Reagan, Ronald, 124

Reed, Richard R., 70
Reynolds, Burt, 124
Richard the Lion-Hearted, King, 91
Robbins, Hargus, 124
Robe, Wolf, 12
Robert the Bruce, King, 123
Rose, S. E. F., 73
Rucker, Edmund W., 124
Scott, George C., 124
Scruggs, Earl, 124
Seabrook, John L., 124
Seabrook, Lochlainn, 123-125
Seger, Bob, 124
Sheibley, Mattie B., 96
Sherman, William T., 12, 29, 61, 63, 64, 96
Simmons, William J., 67, 68, 80
Sitting Bull, 22
Skaggs, Ricky, 124
Stanton, C. A., 102
Stanton, Edwin M., 61, 63, 64
Stephens, Alexander H., 9, 11, 124
Stewart, Alexander P., 124
Streight, Able D., 97
Stuart, Jeb, 124
Taylor, Richard, 11, 57, 90, 124
Taylor, Sarah K., 124
Taylor, Zachary, 124
Tocqueville, Alexis de, 17
Tynes, Ellen B., 124
Vance, Robert B., 124
Vance, Zebulon, 124
Venable, Charles S., 124
Washburn, Cadwallader C., 63
Washington, George, 10
Washington, John A., 124
Washington, Thornton A., 124
Williams, Major, 65
Wilson, Woodrow, 124
Winbush, Nelson W., 48
Winder, Charles S., 124
Winder, John H., 124

Witherspoon, Reese, 124
Wolseley, Garnet J., 97
Womack, John B., 124
Womack, Lee Ann, 124
Wyeth, John A., 89, 91, 93
Young, J. P., 102
Zollicoffer, Felix K., 124

Nathan Bedford Forrest

★★★★★★★★★★★★★★★★★★★★★★★★

ONCE A HERO
ALWAYS A HERO

122   **NATHAN BEDFORD FORREST & AFRICAN-AMERICANS**

ADVERTISEMENT

SEA RAVEN PRESS

IS SUPPORTED & ENDORSED BY AWARD-WINNING WRITER, EDUCATOR, & ARTIST

GREGORY NEWSON

AUTHOR OF
Uncle T and the Uppity Spy

NewsonPublishing.com

MEET THE AUTHOR

"ASKING THE PATRIOTIC SOUTH TO STOP HONORING HER CONFEDERATE ANCESTORS IS LIKE ASKING THE SUN NOT TO SHINE." — COLONEL LOCHLAINN SEABROOK

LOCHLAINN SEABROOK, a Kentucky Colonel and the winner of the prestigious Jefferson Davis Historical Gold Medal for his "masterpiece," *A Rebel Born: A Defense of Nathan Bedford Forrest*, is an unreconstructed Southern historian, award-winning author, Civil War scholar, Bible authority, and traditional Southern Agrarian of Scottish, English, Irish, Dutch, Welsh, German, and Italian extraction.

A child prodigy, Seabrook is today a true Renaissance Man whose occupational titles also include encyclopedist, lexicographer, musician, artist, graphic designer, genealogist, photographer, and award-winning poet. Also a songwriter and a screenwriter, he has a 40 year background in historical nonfiction writing and is a member of the Sons of Confederate Veterans, the Civil War Trust, and the National Grange.

Above, Colonel Lochlainn Seabrook, award-winning Civil War scholar and unreconstructed Southern historian. America's most popular and prolific pro-South author, his many books have introduced hundreds of thousands to the truth about the War for Southern Independence. He coined the phrase "South-shaming" and holds the world's record for writing the most books on Nathan Bedford Forrest: nine.

Due to similarities in their writing styles, ideas, and literary works, Seabrook is often referred to as the "new Shelby Foote," the "Southern Joseph Campbell," and the "American Robert Graves" (his English cousin). Seabrook coined the term "South-shaming," and holds the world's record for writing the most books on Nathan Bedford Forrest: nine. In addition, Seabrook is the first Civil War scholar to connect the early American nickname for the U.S., "The Confederate States of America," with the Southern Confederacy that arose eight decades later, and the first to note that in 1860 the party platforms of the two major political parties were the opposite of what they are today (Victorian Democrats were conservatives, Victorian Republicans were liberals).

The grandson of an Appalachian coal-mining family, Seabrook is a seventh-generation Kentuckian, co-chair of the Jent/Gent Family Committee (Kentucky), founder and director of the Blakeney Family Tree Project, and a board member of the Friends of Colonel Benjamin E. Caudill. Seabrook's literary works have been endorsed by leading authorities, museum curators, award-winning historians, bestselling authors, celebrities, noted scientists, well respected educators, TV show hosts and producers, renowned military artists, esteemed Southern organizations, and distinguished academicians from around the world.

Seabrook has authored over 50 popular adult books on the American Civil War, American and international slavery, the U.S. Confederacy (1781), the Southern Confederacy (1861), religion, theology and thealogy, Jesus, the Bible, the Apocrypha, the Law of Attraction, alternative health, spirituality, ghost stories, the paranormal, ufology, social issues, and cross-cultural studies of the family and marriage. His Confederate biographies, pro-South studies, genealogical monographs, family histories, military encyclopedias, self-help guides, and etymological dictionaries have received wide acclaim.

Seabrook's eight children's books include a Southern guide to the Civil War, a biography of Nathan Bedford Forrest, a dictionary of religion and myth, a rewriting of the King Arthur legend (which reinstates the original pre-Christian motifs), two bedtime stories for preschoolers, a naturalist's guidebook to owls, a worldwide look at the family, and an examination of the Near-Death Experience.

Of blue-blooded Southern stock through his Kentucky, Tennessee, Virginia, West Virginia, and

North Carolina ancestors, he is a direct descendant of European royalty via his 6th great-grandfather, the Earl of Oxford, after which London's famous Harley Street is named. Among his celebrated male Celtic ancestors is Robert the Bruce, King of Scotland, Seabrook's 22nd great-grandfather. The 21st great-grandson of Edward I "Longshanks" Plantagenet), King of England, Seabrook is a thirteenth-generation Southerner through his descent from the colonists of Jamestown, Virginia (1607).

The 2nd, 3rd, and 4th great-grandson of dozens of Confederate soldiers, one of his closest connections to Lincoln's War is through his 3rd great-grandfather, Elias Jent, Sr., who fought for the Confederacy in the Thirteenth Cavalry Kentucky under Seabrook's 2nd cousin, Colonel Benjamin E. Caudill. The Thirteenth, also known as "Caudill's Army," fought in numerous conflicts, including the Battles of Saltville, Gladsville, Mill Cliff, Poor Fork, Whitesburg, and Leatherwood.

Seabrook is a direct descendant of the families of Alexander H. Stephens, John Singleton Mosby, William Giles Harding, and Edmund Winchester Rucker, and is related to the following Confederates and other 18th- and 19th-Century luminaries: Robert E. Lee, Stephen Dill Lee, Stonewall Jackson, Nathan Bedford Forrest, James Longstreet, John Hunt Morgan, Jeb Stuart, Pierre G. T. Beauregard (approved the Confederate Battle Flag design), George W. Gordon, John Bell Hood, Alexander Peter Stewart, Arthur M. Manigault, Joseph Manigault, Charles Scott Venable, Thornton A. Washington, John A. Washington, Abraham Buford, Edmund W. Pettus, Theodrick "Tod" Carter, John B. Womack, John H. Winder, Gideon J. Pillow, States Rights Gist, Henry R. Jackson, John Lawton Seabrook, John C. Breckinridge, Leonidas Polk, Zachary Taylor, Sarah Knox Taylor (first wife of Jefferson Davis), Richard Taylor, Davy Crockett, Daniel Boone, Meriwether Lewis (of the Lewis and Clark Expedition) Andrew Jackson, James K. Polk, Abram Poindexter Maury (founder of Franklin, TN), Zebulon Vance, Thomas Jefferson, Edmund Jennings Randolph, George Wythe Randolph (grandson of Jefferson), Felix K. Zollicoffer, Fitzhugh Lee, Nathaniel F. Cheairs, Jesse James, Frank James, Robert Brank Vance, Charles Sidney Winder, John W. McGavock, Caroline E. (Winder) McGavock, David Harding McGavock, Lysander McGavock, James Randal McGavock, Randal William McGavock, Francis McGavock, Emily McGavock, William Henry F. Lee, Lucius E. Polk, Minor Meriwether (husband of noted pro-South author Elizabeth Avery Meriwether), Ellen Bourne Tynes (wife of Forrest's chief of artillery, Captain John W. Morton), South Carolina Senators Preston Smith Brooks and Andrew Pickens Butler, and famed South Carolina diarist Mary Chesnut.

Seabrook's modern day cousins include: Patrick J. Buchanan (conservative author), Cindy Crawford (model), Shelby Lee Adams (Letcher Co., Kentucky, photographer), Bertram Thomas Combs (Kentucky's 50th governor), Edith Bolling (wife of President Woodrow Wilson), and actors Andy Griffith, George C. Scott, Robert Duvall, Reese Witherspoon, Lee Marvin, Rebecca Gayheart, and Tom Cruise.

Seabrook's screenplay, *A Rebel Born*, based on his book of the same name, has been signed with acclaimed filmmaker Christopher Forbes (of Forbes Film). It is now in pre-production, and is set for release in 2017 as a full-length feature film. This will be the first movie ever made of Nathan Bedford Forrest's life story, and as a historically accurate project written from the Southern perspective, is destined to be one of the most talked about Civil War films of all time.

Born with music in his blood, Seabrook is an award-winning, multi-genre, BMI-Nashville songwriter and lyricist who has composed some 3,000 songs (250 albums), and whose original music has been heard in film (*A Rebel Born*, *Cowgirls 'n Angels*, *Confederate Cavalry*, *Billy the Kid: Showdown in Lincoln County*, *Vengeance Without Mercy*, *Last Step*, *County Line*, *The Mark*) and on TV and radio worldwide. A musician, producer, multi-instrumentalist, and renown performer—whose keyboard work has been variously compared to pianists from Hargus Robbins and Vince Guaraldi to Elton John and Leonard Bernstein—Seabrook has opened for groups such as the Earl Scruggs Review, Ted Nugent, and Bob Seger, and has performed privately for such public figures as President Ronald Reagan, Burt Reynolds, Loni Anderson, and Senator Edward W. Brooke. Seabrook's cousins in the music business include: Johnny Cash, Elvis Presley, Billy Ray and Miley Cyrus, Patty Loveless, Tim McGraw, Lee Ann Womack, Dolly Parton, Pat Boone, Naomi, Wynonna, and Ashley Judd, Ricky Skaggs, the Sunshine Sisters, Martha Carson, and Chet Atkins.

Seabrook lives with his wife and family in historic Middle Tennessee, the heart of Forrest country and the Confederacy, where his conservative Southern ancestors fought valiantly against Liberal Lincoln and the progressive North in defense of Jeffersonianism, constitutional government, and personal liberty.

LochlainnSeabrook.com

LOCHLAINN SEABROOK   125

If you enjoyed this book you will be interested in Colonel Seabrook's other popular related titles:

☛ EVERYTHING YOU WERE TAUGHT ABOUT THE CIVIL WAR IS WRONG, ASK A SOUTHERNER!
☛ EVERYTHING YOU WERE TAUGHT ABOUT AMERICAN SLAVERY IS WRONG, ASK A SOUTHERNER!
☛ CONFEDERATE FLAG FACTS: WHAT EVERY AMERICAN SHOULD KNOW ABOUT DIXIE'S SOUTHERN CROSS
☛ CONFEDERACY 101: AMAZING FACTS YOU NEVER KNEW ABOUT AMERICA'S OLDEST POLITICAL TRADITION

Available from Sea Raven Press and wherever fine books are sold

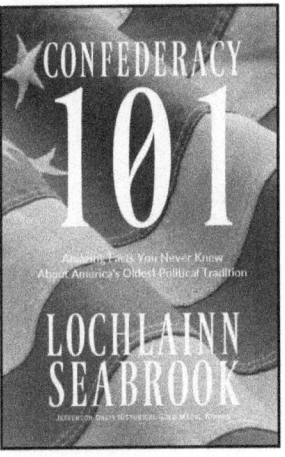

ALL OF OUR BOOK COVERS ARE AVAILABLE AS 11" X 17" POSTERS, SUITABLE FOR FRAMING.

SeaRavenPress.com • NathanBedfordForrestBooks.com